15.95

HOW TO OVERCOME YOUR SECRET FEAR OF

FAILURE

RECOGNIZING AND BEATING YOUR 'ACHILLES SYNDROME'

Professor Petrūska Clarkson of PHYSIS, London, fellow of the British
Association for Counselling and Fellow of the British Psychological Society
has written many books and papers, and is a Consultant Psychologist,
Psychotherapist Supervisor and Management Consultant working and
teaching at universities and private institutions internationally.

To Edna – the best teacher of my life

HOW TO OVERCOME YOUR SECRET FEAR OF
FAILURE

RECOGNIZING AND BEATING YOUR 'ACHILLES SYNDROME'

Petrūska Clarkson

First published by Element Books Ltd 1994
© Vega 2003
Text © Petrūska Clarkson 1994

ISBN 1 84333 157 8
A catalogue record for this book is available from the British Library

Published in 2003 by Vega, 64 Brewery Road, London, N7 9NT
Visit our website at www.chrysalisbooks.co.uk

A member of Chrysalis Books plc

AUG 2 9 2003

Jacket design: Grade Design Consultants
Managing Editor: Laurence Henderson
Production: Susan Sutterby

Printed in Great Britain by
Creative Print and Design Wales

Contents

Tables and Figures

Acknowledgements

I am grateful to many people who assisted in bringing this work to fruition; among them Hella Adler, Vincent Keyter and Elana Leigh. I also extend my gratitude to those who read and commented on the manuscript, especially Muriel James, Geoff Mead, Denton Roberts, John Rowan and Patricia Shaw for their detailed and helpful suggestions.

I also wish to thank Julia McCutchen for all help and encouragement as editor, and Edwina Welham for her early support. I am deeply grateful to Katherine Pierpoint, in particular, who has cared for this creation with imagination, patience and diligence, ably supported by Camilla Sim. Many people contributed examples; also clients, trainers, trainees, supervisors and supervisees, friends and colleagues who have shared their lives with me and taught me so much about the pain of this experience as well as the pleasures and satisfactions of overcoming it.

The extract from *Arcadia* by Tom Stoppard (1993) on pp. 167–8 is reprinted with permission from Faber and Faber.

The extracts at the start of each chapter are reprinted from *The Iliad* by Homer (1950 edition), translated by E.V. Rieu, with permission from Penguin Books.

Preface

This book describes the Achilles Syndrome. It is forged from the experience of people who are acknowledged as winners but feel like losers.

It brings together information from child-development theory, the psychology of myths in everyday life and theories of how people learn, as well as practical exercises on how to heal oneself and others. In my teaching and counselling I work from a basic assumption that human beings have, along with sexual and aggressive drives, an equally important instinct to fulfil their own potential – a drive for evolutionary development through creativity, achieving competence and striving for excellence in their lives. This human instinct is only recognized by relatively few psychologists – those who believe that humankind has the capacity and the desire to create a better future than the past it has inherited. The desire to become good at whatever it is we do, and then even better, is a powerful motivating force. This need has been called 'self-actualization'.[1] I identify it with the instinct for creative evolution which ancient philosophers such as Zeno called *Physis*.[2] Physis has been called the creative force of nature – the life force itself – which 'eternally strives to make things grow and to make growing things more perfect'.[3]

When people try to become competent or excellent in their lives or respective fields, I believe they do so in response to this internal creative drive called Physis. Pseudocompetency refers to the times or areas where Physis has been blocked, damaged or perverted. It can occur in individual or organizational lives. And Physis is ever changing; change must occur because change is life. I do not ever consider 'doing' more important than 'being' or existing, as if competency were the be-all and end-all of existence. However, being competent is a very significant aspect of life achievement and satisfaction. Most human beings not only want to live and love well but also want to work well. I consider this desire for growth and development vital for individual health and collective survival, and I work to create an environment in myself and others where Physis can grow.

Some people may want to read this book from beginning to end, others may want to skip around in it finding sections which take their fancy. I have added exercises and experiments at the end of each chapter as stimulation points for you to use, change or ignore. They are intended to be used at people's own pace and discretion. Everybody is uniquely different and what works for one temperament may have the opposite effect on someone else or on you in another mood. It is also possible to misinterpret or abuse any form of self-help advice. Please be careful to treat information, yourself and others with respect and compassion. If you feel that it would be better if you seek professional help from a counsellor or psychotherapist, then do so. Directories of counsellors and psychotherapists and/or referral systems are available from the British Association of Counselling and the United Kingdom Council for Psychotherapy.

The material in this book is based on the true stories of many people describing how pseudocompetency affected their lives and occasionally how they succeeded in achieving true competency. My motivation is to help ordinary people understand this far-reaching syndrome and, in doing so, to help make some principles of psychology available to all, not just kept to the experts.

Although this book is my own work, it is obviously the end result of more than two decades of learning and reading. This experience of the fields of psychology, psychotherapy, philosophy, sociology, literature and others has formed the fertilized ground from which this book has emerged. Wherever possible, specific contributions have been acknowledged in the listed references. My apologies for any unintentional oversights.

I have sought written permission to use the extended examples. I rarely use a shorter example which I have only come across once. Thus, even if you do think you recognize yourself or think you recognize someone else, a. it is unlikely that you are alone, and b. I usually use composites (that is, I put together different facets of stories in order to protect people's privacy). All names and identifying details have, of course, been changed to protect the confidentiality of these people involved in learning about the Achilles Syndrome and contributing to our understanding of how to resolve it. I am particularly grateful to the reader who told me at an Achilles workshop: 'The blurb seemed to be the story of my life.' Without such frequent heartfelt recognition and people's feedback on its usefulness in their lives, I would not have done the hard work of writing this book. I could also have spent a lifetime researching this complex issue further. Instead, this book exists by popular demand to make the material public by those who have already found the workshops useful. This book is offered in the knowledge that it could of course be better, but nonetheless in its present form can still be valuable as fodder for our own experimentation and imagination. People are therefore invited to create something from it for themselves.

As this book was going to press a colleague brought it to my attention that a similar idea has been written about before in the form of *The Impostor Phenomenon*.[4] Although I have not read the material except as reported in an article in *Time*[5] magazine (the book is out of print), I would like to acknowledge Clance and Harvey for their precedence in this area. From what I can tell, the idea of pseudocompetency is probably different from the Impostor Phenomenon since it centres around gaps or skips in the learning cycle rather than primarily the experience of being a fraud. For example, in Chapter 12 I talk about the pseudocompetency of modern society toward the environment, which is difficult to think about purely in terms of people feeling that they are impostors.

Far from being disappointed that someone else seems to have been on the case, I welcome it as a reinforcement that others have also thought along these lines, identifying this syndrome and helping uncover it for everyone's benefit. It constantly reassures me that the pattern we are investigating exists in an understood and recognizable way for so many people. I hope readers can enjoy and continue to learn from all possible sources in growing more effective and confident in their work, and to increase their enjoyment of life.

There is much that I can say which will exceed the space here. Please accept hints, read further if you want and imagine or find a friend or colleague with whom to work out any parts with which you disagree or about which you would like to know more. I know that the delivery of this manuscript is but one place in my learning cycle about the Achilles Syndrome – soon I shall know less, or begin to learn what I still need to learn again.

Suggestions

- You have probably bought or borrowed this book because you recognized some aspects of this pattern in yourself (or in someone close to you). So you will perhaps read this book wishing to find some answers, overcome some problems or clarify some confusion about your competency in whatever field – whether it is gardening, planning the Christmas meal or delivering a speech in Parliament. It is important for human beings to have aspirations and to strive for pleasure and excellence. It does not have to be the same as an endless and self-punishing demand for perfection. You could do the following experiment which may enhance the value you get out of this book.
- Set yourself three goals now and be willing to write them down. Picture vividly, like a film screen, how you would look and feel accomplishing your goals. Imagine that your inner sense of confidence lies easy in your heart and body as you execute your desired goal. Be prepared to have

achieved them by the time you reach the end of this book. Take care with this and choose things that are important to you, rather than trying to achieve other people's objectives – for this reason I am not making suggestions. By all means be optimistic and positive, but make them realistic.

Once you are clear in your mind that you truly want to achieve these three objectives and know you can do it, start to plan the steps along the way that will lead to accomplishing them. How will you know that you have achieved them? What are the first steps you can put in place now?

CHAPTER ONE

The Secret Flaw

THE ACHILLES SYNDROME – PSEUDOCOMPETENCY

*Look at me. Am I not big and beautiful, the son of a great man, with a
Goddess for my Mother? But Death and sovran Destiny are waiting
for me too. A morning is coming, or maybe an evening or a noon, when
somebody is going to kill me too in battle with a cast of his spear or an
arrow from his bow. (p. 383)*

Introduction

In this chapter I introduce the concept of the Achilles Syndrome, which I have technically called pseudocompetency.
This is followed by an exploration of the archetypal roots
of this problem as found in Homer's ancient tale of Achilles,
the Greek hero. Such ancient myths and legends can help
us understand the nature of some human difficulties and
yearnings at a more profound level.

The Achilles Pattern of Modern People

In the early 1970s my consultancy, counselling and psychotherapy practice began to attract many people who were high
achievers, often around the top of their respective fields, but
who suffered from a serious lack of self-esteem. They had
been acknowledged by others as 'winners' but inside they
felt like losers. The problem seemed to revolve around their

competence, or effectiveness in the world – a mismatch between their abilities and their confidence.

These sensitive, successful, and creative people had good basic psychological functioning. Many had good healthy working lives with interesting friendship and family networks. They had few of the psychiatric difficulties which can incapacitate people or need hospital treatment. Although, like many human beings, they had some deep-seated scars or left-over emotional issues from childhood, their main desire was to grow as personalities and develop their creative potential. This group appeared even more successful than average, but there was always a worm in the apple of their success. They carried much anxiety about the fact that the way they felt was not matched by the praise which their world only too eagerly bestowed. Although uniquely different as individuals, their discomfort seemed to have a noticeably common shape. I had begun to discover the syndrome of pseudocompetency.

I began to identify a particular pattern of physical, psychological and social factors common to these gifted or just ordinary people. The world saw them as successful whilst they, inside themselves, could not own this success. They could not allow themselves to be nourished by and satisfied with the 'rave review', the straight 'A's', the 'glowing report'. A particular combination of distressing factors seemed to recur again and again, eating away at their self-esteem and gnawing at their faith in their own futures. They were smarting under a psychological injury. This wound had not been effectively healed even in previous counselling or therapeutic experiences. It had to do with the basic human need not just to act competent, but to be seen as and to feel competent. I tried to understand it. I went back to my textbooks and teachers. But I could not trace anyone else at the time who had identified this syndrome in the way that I seemed to be meeting it day after day in my consulting room, on counselling training programmes and when consulting to organizations. Theories or practical psychological help which focused on creativity and competence were few and far between. When discussing this with one of the best teachers of my life – Edna Deudney – she suggested that Achilles seems to be the archetypal image for this condition – Achilles the almost invincible Greek hero of the Trojan Wars who had a vulnerable heel.

The story of Achilles with his fatal flaw was present in many of the lives of my clients. *John,* for example, was an attractive 35-year-old executive in an advertising agency when he was first referred to me for counselling. As far as his career was concerned he has done very well, earning a large salary. He also has a relatively happy home life. He has a reputation as a high-flying 'whizz-kid' in his work and has on several occasions masterminded the campaign presentations that have landed the company with some major accounts. John has received lots of recognition and praise for his excellence and is so well regarded by colleagues and superiors that he has been made a partner well ahead of his professional peers. On the surface there is no reason why he should not be very satisfied and happy with himself and his achievements. However, *he feels* that his success is all very precarious. In his words:

> I get sick with anxiety before I lead the team to make any major presentation. I throw up; I feel as if I am quite incapable of doing it successfully; I fear that this time people will 'see through me' – I will be shamed in front of everybody. I have fantasies that clients and colleagues may suddenly see me for the fraud I feel I am. I feel I've 'duped' people all along; 'fooled' them into thinking better of me than is real.
>
> I often desperately try to remember past successes and reassure myself that I can repeat them, but I can't convince myself and I have the sneaking suspicion that all my previous achievements were 'flukes'. When I manage to 'bamboozle' the others into believing that I am better than I am, I don't seem to be able to carry the feeling of success from my achievements from the past into the future.
>
> No matter how small the presentation I always seem to feel as if it's not just my performance, but my very self that's on the line. I fear that someone in the audience will one day jump up and call me the fraud that I feel I am. In my nightmares I often

see people suddenly finding out that I am not wearing the right clothes, or that I don't really know the group password. My salary keeps rising and I get more and more praise, but in myself I get more and more anxious, and I drink more and more. I cannot shake off this constant tension. I see people who are less competent and apparently less successful than I am and I envy them the pleasure they get from their work, the buzz of excitement when they look forward to a new challenging job, the sense of achievement and enhanced self-confidence afterwards.

None of the friends I've tried to tell about how I feel can understand what I am uncomfortable about. They say I am falsely modest or I 'just' lack self-confidence. I try to give myself credit where credit is due but it just does not seem real. The very thought of the next presentation just brings me out in a cold sweat and the genuine gut-wrenching fear that I won't pull it off.

Sally is a young career woman who manages to keep an efficient, welcoming home. With her husband Tom, she is bringing up two lovely children. To the outside world she seems to keep all these balls quite successfully in the air. Other people call her competent, even talented, but her counsellor (whom she went to because of tranquilliser addiction) knows that Sally suffers from deep and profound self-doubt, never sure in herself that she can be as competent and efficient tomorrow as she was yesterday. As a child, Sally was too young for her class and struggled to keep up, but every year she was put in the next class because she just managed to pass. No one noticed the strain, the nightmares and the lack of pleasure in learning and achievement which became her way of life.

Tommy is an exceptionally bright and gifted 10 year old who does very well at school. Neither his teachers nor his family can understand why he bites his nails, lies awake worrying at night, and always fears that he has failed before his exam results come out. Everybody *knows* that Tommy *always gets distinctions*. When he does well people say, 'We expected you to get a distinction.' However, it is only Tommy himself who fears that he may not pass or that even when he does he has somehow 'fooled' his teachers into believing that he knows more or is better at his subject than he himself believes. Tommy lives in quite a pleasant family with no serious problems so everybody from parents to school psychologists find it very hard to understand why he remains so anxious and tense and has so little pleasure from his school work when he is actually, according to all objective criteria, so *good* at it. We have all read newspaper reports or even been affected by the examples of academically bright kids with excellent records who unaccountably commit suicide just before their exams. Tommy could be one of those if he does not get help and understanding.

These are quite common examples of people who are thought of *by others* as competent, gifted, or even exceptionally talented. However, they all feel that in some way they have a secret flaw or inadequacy which, if exposed, would make it humiliatingly clear to everyone that they were not as good as they were made out to be. Against all the evidence, they doubt their abilities. In each case there is a fundamental *discrepancy* between people's *own* sense of their competence or worth and the perception of *others* of this competency. There is a sense in which they fear that they are always covering up some secret but fatal flaw, even though they might not quite know what this is. They feel they are at the mercy of a particularly perceptive, cynical or critical judge who could call their bluff any day and expose them as the impostors they feel they are. The emotion they fear most of all is shame – the public humiliation which they fear will inevitably follow if their secret inadequacy were to be exposed to public view. An experienced teacher told me that if anyone in his class were to find out that he did not know an answer, he would 'die of shame. Just disappear down a hole'.

A Feeling of Phoney Excellence

Some people's whole lives are designed around building up extensive 'psychological armour' to make up for a profound sense of flawedness or inadequacy. They are often described

as 'having a chip on their shoulder'. For others pseudocompetency may manifest in only some isolated areas of their life.
Some people may sometimes be maimed by it or – at the
other extreme – psycho-logically destroyed. Whether it concerns the whole personality or some specific areas, people
hide it more or less effectively. Some may even appear to be
self-confident and relaxed but are internally tormented with
self-doubt and anxiety before they accomplish the tasks at
which they are considered by others to be already excellent.
After having done the performance, given the speech, talked
to the children about sex, or finally achieved an effortful
orgasm, they feel exhausted, drained, burnt out. The effort
of having achieved, and the subsequent depletion and strain,
robs their experience of all possible pleasure and minimizes
or deletes the positive appreciation for their performance
which they received from other people. The standing ova-
tion, the praising review, the salary increase, is not reflected
in a similar rise in self-esteem. In fact people may even find
such positive feedback oppressive. For example, having bril-
liantly won a squash competition for his club, a sportsman
said with anxiety instead of exhilaration in his voice, 'Now
they'll expect me to be that good every time'.

Most people have one or more areas in which they feel that
they 'overachieve'. These are areas in which other people
(who are usually competent judges in the relevant field)
consider them to be excellent or very good. However, in their
own heart of hearts, they sometimes fear that they cannot
genuinely 'own' the praise. They do not allow themselves to
be nourished by these other people's appreciation. They feel
that they never really deserve the accolades they receive, and
even if they did, they cannot be even reasonably certain that
they will be able to repeat that success in the future. Their
sense of competence feels as if it is built on sand, always
subject to threat, to exposure, to shame, and to public humiliation. When the performance is over, there is only the
relief that 'This time I've not been found out. What a lucky
break – I've been able to hide the shortfall between what
people have come to expect of me and what I actually feel I

can deliver. I have escaped being shamed this time . . . but it feels like a house of cards. Will I get away with it next time?'

Such a mismatch between subjective and objective judgement may seem irrational and unbelievable to observers. Although they may deny it, the sufferers are often talented, gifted or intelligent people. The fear of the public exposure seems quite out of proportion. The distress these people experience may often appear incredible to their friends, family and colleagues. How can this self-doubt persist so tenaciously in the face of such repeated external positive feedback? These people themselves feel puzzled and perplexed by it. They may even start to blame themselves for the fact that they can't seem to be able to use their agents', supervisors' or students' praise in a consistent way to maintain or build their self-esteem and trust in their own competencies or gifts. Their friends may even get impatient because their appreciation is so minimized; it seems as if the person just cannot use it positively in a consistent way. A further irony is that they are not necessarily the kind of people who would usually seek psychological help. Some people end up psychologically 'crippled' by this phenomenon, others are 'hamstrung' by it in one way or another. It can infect a whole life.

Old Myths, New Headlines

Sometimes ancient myths or stories can provide us with images or metaphors which illuminate recurrent human dilemmas or problems. Learning from and thinking about life's problems through identifying with the characters in stories, legends and even today's films is a potent human way of trying to make sense and meaning of our lives and getting help in solving our dilemmas. Jung's[1] ideas of archetypes are of this nature. Archetypes can be described as inherited patterns of meaning dating from our earliest ancestors and supposed to be present in us as potential images or meanings which can be realized in individual lives. They are often carried in myths. Myths or ancient stories influence our everyday consciousness in very important ways. The story of the publicly acclaimed person who secretly knows that he/she is covering up a flaw which may prove fatal to him/her is well known in ancient legends. Achilles is one such story. We also frequently read about similar stories in today's newspapers – the secret sexual vice of an evangelical preacher, the hidden drug addiction of a family doctor. It may have been part of human consciousness since the time people first started reflecting on the meaning of their lives, and it is still with us. Studying these ancient myths can sometimes illustrate and help us in our lives today.

The Story of Achilles

Achilles was the Greek hero who seemed immortal and won every battle, but who had a secret and fatal vulnerability. I use him as an image for all people who may feel that, in some way, their achievements are a pretence and that they are covering up this secret without being able to tell others.

Achilles' Mother: Thetis

Thetis, the most celebrated of the Nereids (sea nymphs) was due to marry Zeus. But a seer prophesied that Thetis would give birth to a man more powerful than his father, and so Zeus prudently decided to marry her to a mortal. He chose Peleus, King of Thessaly. Thetis was offended at being put amongst the mortals, and attempted to escape from Peleus by taking on various shapes: she changed herself into a fish, then an animal, a fluid wave, and then burning flame. Thanks to the advice of the centaur Chiron, Peleus finally won her and their marriage was celebrated with great pomp in the presence of the gods, who showered handsome gifts on the couple. Eventually Thetis returned to the Nereids.

Achilles' Father: Peleus

King Peleus was one of the most famous heroes of Thessaly, who had a wild and battle-filled struggle to gain the throne. He killed King Acastus, nearly getting killed himself in the attempt on a dangerous boar-hunting expedition, but was saved by the centaur Chiron. Soon afterwards Peleus married Thetis, and Achilles was born from their union. Peleus was an absent father. While his son grew up, Peleus had many adventures, sailing with the Argonauts and waging many more heroic battles. He outlived his son and had a listless old age.

Achilles

Although this story has several versions, the one I will use here tells that Thetis was ambitious for her baby son. She wanted to ensure Achilles' immortality and give him wonderful, extra-human qualities. The river Styx was one of the nine rivers of the ancient underworld which could bestow immortality on human beings. In order to make Achilles immortal, Thetis plunged him in the Styx. In this way she made his body invulnerable except for the heel by which she held him. Doing this would make him immortal like a god and immune to physical injury. However his heel, being untouched by this process, remained the vulnerable, mortal part of Achilles, the place where he could be fatally injured if only others could see through the deception to his fatal hidden flaw.

As long as his secret remained hidden, Achilles was safe from death and secure that he was invincible in his field of excellence – battle. He was an amazing warrior, yet also a great healer. He moved within a cycle of alternate destruction and healing, also healing the people he had wounded. But if his secret shame was exposed he would be at the mercy of any enemy – not necessarily the strongest or the smartest one, but anyone who would use his secret flaw against him.

Achilles was thus *'passing for'* immortal. Complete identification with the Achilles archetype renders people false heroes, and they do not learn how to break the trap by using the best response or defending themselves in more effective ways.

In a similar way some coloured people in South Africa sometimes tried to escape the punitive race laws by passing for white. This meant that a child who 'looked white' would go and live with a white family, attend a white school, and avoid or deny their true family of origin. Their parents were usually trying to get them better opportunities in an unjust society, but it comes at the cost of tears, deception and constant fear. A thorough look at the complexity of such fraught historical and social situations is beyond the scope of this book. The natural and justifiable human desire to free ourselves from the constraints of restrictive laws (or mortality) is an inescapable psychological yearning. Survival choices may always be at the risk of public exposure and the loss of all privileges associated with desirable status, whether that be colour or immortality. Of course, nobody can be free if hostage to another's approval, whether it be for external reasons such as colour or internal reasons such as value judgements.

Reading Homer's story, we can easily imagine that Achilles was very concerned about putting on the appropriate armour to protect his heel from attack in battle. Hephaestus, goldsmith to the gods themselves, made his armour. Yet every time Achilles went into battle, he knew that he had this potentially fatal secret – that he could be killed by an injury to his heel. Naturally Achilles would take great care to 'cover up' this inadequacy which betrayed his status as an 'immortal' – a man who could not be killed. So while, on the one hand, he was a glorious, apparently invincible warrior, on the other hand it was actually very easy to kill him if only the enemy knew the exact spot at which to point the arrow or the spear. This goes a long way towards explaining why Achilles' psychology was so complex – almost as complex as that of the modern 'captain of industry', 'high-flying woman executive', or 'Superwoman',[2] who juggles motherhood, a demanding career and complex marriage. How many people feel like that: strong, powerful and sure of themselves at one level, and yet scared that someone will find and use the chink in their armour.

Achilles combines many apparently irreconcilable polarities in the story of his life. As a youngster he was given over to the centaur Chiron who fed him on the marrowbones of bears and the entrails of lions to give him courage. Chiron taught Achilles the arts of healing, riding, hunting, and playing the pipes and lyre. He is reported to have loved both women and men. He fought valiantly in battle for his country, but was also considered a traitor by the common people. It is told that he sulked in cowardly sullenness, refusing to fight when his pride was slighted, but also that he conquered even the fabulously famed strong man Hector the Trojan in single combat. He exacted the most terrible revenge for the betrayal and killing of his friends and was a loyal and trusted ally of other great Greek warriors. He was a mortal, but his myth is universal.

Achilles was thus a major hero of his time, even though he died from his fatal flaw. Either Paris or Apollo (versions vary) ended his life with a poisoned spear, having taken advantage of (or betrayed) Achilles' momentary, inadvertent lack of heel protection. This notion of longing and fear encapsulated in the fatal, secret vulnerability of Achilles has clearly resonated in us since our ancestors' oral histories began. The blind poet Homer (quoted at the beginning of this chapter) is only one of many storytellers to dramatize his story.

The Achilles Syndrome

There is much more to be said about Achilles, and about the meaning of his legend for the Achilles types of our time. However, this brief sketch will have to serve as a classical introduction to what I have come to term the 'Achilles Syndrome'. The power of the Achilles legend still lives on in the popular imagination today. We all have a sense of the meaning of the commonly used phrase '*Achilles' heel*' and its link with vulnerability. The archetypal evocation of the idea of the Achilles' heel (as something which any of us may have) is very significant to people of the twentieth century as we try to achieve integrity between what is expected of us and what we can actually deliver. Understanding the legend could help us to accept and begin to deal with the problems of the ordinary or exceptional individual trapped in a self-imposed pretence which may lead to endless emotional torment or a tragic end.

In my many years as a psychotherapist, counsellor, supervisor and organizational consultant, I have been in contact with numerous people suffering from a kind of Achilles Syndrome. These people are seen by others as much more competent than they feel in themselves, and they exert inappropriate amounts of energy and tension to perform, or are exhausted and drained by success instead of it building up their confidence. They may develop defences to cover up what they feel is their 'Achilles' heel'. The defences may end up as limitations and unnecessary handicaps. Furthermore the sufferers may over-compensate by becoming more and more acknowledged in their field, all the while still fearing the exposure of the part they feel they have always hidden from view.

The terms pseudocompetency or the Achilles Syndrome are different from competence and incompetence, as I will show shortly. It must also be differentiated from self-criticism, which is often a disguised attack on one's self-esteem stemming from the influence of parents or harsh, punitive educational practices. It may of course be fed and supported by negative messages from any impatient person in one's life. Parents or teachers may also give injunctions; taboos or prohibitions which can hurt or damage a person's life by forbidding them to ask questions, call for help or seek appropriate protection.

In a similar way many heroes of our time – the people who are commonly considered to be excellent or gifted –

are often covering up some potentially embarrassing flaw. There may be a head of state who does not really understand the term 'Gross National Product'. Maybe a mother develops a reputation for efficiency and competency based on her performance as leader of the parent-teachers' association. But she finds it all such a strain that she has to drink half a bottle of gin before she can, apparently effortlessly, undertake any of these public engagements. Another flawed individual may be the internationally acclaimed, Oscar-winning actor who is paralysed with stage-fright every night before he faces the footlights, fearing that *this time* he will forget his lines and his beloved audience will fall out of love with him. There are 'experts' in every field who are covering up more or less consciously. Who they are, none but their own hearts will know. Whereas the Achilles Syndrome is the more poetic name for this particular brand of human suffering, pseudocompetency is the more psychologically technical term. You may of course want to invent a better term for yourself.

What is Pseudocompetency?

Pseudocompetency refers to the experience of a big difference between people's own (low) assessment of themselves and others' (high) opinion of them in their particular field. We are pseudocompetent in this sense when there is a mismatch between our own self-confidence in a particular field and our competence in it as assessed by others. This causes the discomfort or distress many people experience when the internal and external assessments are very dissimilar or contradictory.

Competence means being able to tackle a task well, both subjectively (as assessed by self) *and* objectively (assessed by others). Competence means your inner confidence is well-matched with your performance. *Incompetence* is used here, not as an insult, but as a pointer that further development is needed in order to meet objective competency criteria. It means that you don't yet know how to perform well in the particular area. Acknowledging incompetence here means the beginning of learning is possible.

The flaw in the Achilles person is frequently resistant to cure because there is usually some grain of truth in the person's subjective assessment of inadequacy. There is often a basic existential dishonesty involved – some major or minor way in which the person has avoided mastering some skill, knowledge or attitude in relation to his or her field of excellence. Due to a variety of factors they continue to reap the rewards of high status in the field while neglecting to go back to basics and retrieve the parts they skipped over in their initial learning process.

People with pseudocompetency problems would sometimes (consciously or unconsciously) *like* to have it exposed. Perhaps then they can get understanding of and help for the problem of the vulnerable heel. However, these people usually also fear a potentially humiliating and shaming exposure of this flaw which has been so perfectly concealed from their previous teachers and current admirers.

I furthermore identify *pseudocompetency* as having two parts, relating to the present and the future. The description above is about the present. In the second part, which affects the future, people may appear *objectively* to be able to do the task competently, but *subjectively* do not experience the confidence that they will be able to keep doing it well in future without severe anxiety and without strain or undue energy drainage afterwards. For example, Tony, a public speaker, can command astronomical fees for public appearances since he is so highly regarded as an entertaining speaker. However, before any speech he is filled with appalling self-doubt, anxiety and distress, and is convinced that he is totally incapable of 'delivering the goods' which others have come to expect from him. He feels he cannot do it ever again no matter how many successful performances he accomplishes. He can now at least bring himself to talk about this to a person he feels he can trust and who can help him.

Pseudocompetency is different from competence, and from incompetence. In the way that I am thinking about it here, incompetent means 'not qualified or able to perform a particular task or function . . . showing a lack of skill . . . not able to perform its function'. Competent is defined as 'adequately qualified or capable . . . effective.' Both these dictionary definitions focus on qualification or capability. The implication is that competency can be externally assessed, for example, by getting a driving licence by successfully passing the required test.

Part of competency, particularly as it is used in the helping professions (such as counselling), includes knowing the limits of one's competence; what you can't do or don't know. Competence also has to do with knowing what it is you know and what it is you can do, in self- and externally agreed terms. For example, a competent general practitioner will know when to refer a patient to a specialist consultant with particular competency in dealing with, for example, stomach problems. Counsellors who are specially trained in working with alcoholics can be professionally recognized as competent when they are aware of their shortcomings. Then they can acknowledge the limitations of their capabilities and make the appropriate referral to somebody who *is* competent to treat alcoholics.

Competence therefore implies the knowledge that someone can make a genuine assessment of their capabilities and inabilities. A person is incompetent when they do not meet established criteria, and this needs to be clear to themselves and others. Pseudocompetency happens when this boundary is blurred – when there is uncertainty about whether a person is competent or incompetent according to their own judgement. When a surgeon is not sure if he or she is competent to operate, or a barrister feels inadequate in summing up for the defence, they are no longer genuinely competent.

The mark of a genuinely competent professional is to know what they can and cannot do, as well as being able to judge the competency of their peers and colleagues in the same professional group. Without such commonly agreed criteria for competency there would be no way of distinguishing between good and bad judges, beauticians or insurance brokers – all of whom, if competent and ethical, usually belong to a professional organization which agrees and monitors *competency criteria*. Pseudocompetency is the term I have specifically chosen to capture some of the confusions or ambiguity when internal experience and externally assessed criteria are different or confusing. It is a specifically psychological term, not meant to be used in a demeaning way. It is intended to describe a specific pattern of human distress in the crossover areas of competency and incompetency; an image from a story which can be helpful for people to understand themselves better and to live and love and work with more joy.

What it is Not

So we can see that people who suffer from pseudocompetency are most commonly considered competent people in their respective fields. They are often so bright that they know where their flaws are. It is usually gifted people who can use their talents to cover up for so long. They know what is actually expected, and then know how they can cover it up. Creating a façade for others is in itself a gift – an outcome of creativity applied to a difficult or intolerable situation. One man told me how his father died and he took over the running of the household when he was twelve. He found he had a gift for it and was much praised as 'mummy's little man', looking after the other children and in most respects acting as her stand-in husband. At his twelfth birthday party there was no one else there under the age of 30! He always felt older than his peers, reached high and responsible positions very quickly but carried within himself a deep despair and painful longing for the childhood he had never had.

When we hesitantly admit that we don't feel as competent as others think we are, other people usually won't believe it or take us seriously. We then feel even more foolish and ashamed. We may realize that it would only make the other person feel more uncomfortable if we kept insisting upon our inner truth. When a bright young student who regularly gets top marks for essays tries to tell her teachers that she doesn't really understand the subject, so can't feel confident that she could repeat her achievements effortlessly, her teachers usually say: 'Of course you do understand this, you just don't give yourself enough credit' or 'You just lack self-esteem.' The person who is 'not heard' may then feel even more confused, since their own assessment is so out of line with that of the others.

People who are pseudocompetent are usually neither failures nor braggarts, since failures will tend to be found out quickly and will not, over a long time, manage to uphold a reputation of excellence in their field. Braggarts tend to claim to do more than they really can. Their reputation often is not built on what they have actually done, because they will tend to avoid taking the test, completing the book, entering into the competition. They are more likely to say: 'I could have created a million-dollar company if only I were willing to soil my hands with politics'; 'I too have my bright ideas for books, but my family is too important for me to sacrifice them for fame', or some similar 'rationalization'. *Braggarts tend to feel like winners and behave like losers, whereas failures feel and behave like losers.* The Achilles Syndrome specifically describes those people who *look like winners but feel like losers.* All these terms are here used metaphorically defined by people's own criteria, for every person knows what is right for him or her.

Usually competent people know what the general standard of performance should be and how they fall short of this standard. They are competent enough to have the perspective to know what things should or could be like, and what to do about getting up to standard. It is not the same thing as perfectionism or setting unattainable goals, although these may be mixed up in it. Pseudocompetency is also different from incompetence. Incompetence in a factory line or a farming community, for example, is very easily identified, whereas incompetent counsellors and psychotherapists may never be 'found out'; particularly if they avoid ever taping their work for their peers to listen to.

Pseudocompetency is also not the same as deliberate lying or deception. There have been several people who successfully bluffed their way to working as hospital surgeons who never even went to medical school! Intelligent illiterates develop an enormous capacity to hide their inability to read. Unbelievable though it may seem, a senior executive made a successful career for himself despite being unable to recognize or remember faces. The acuteness of the problem came to light when he was arrested for molesting an elderly woman in the street. He had taken her by the arm and greeted her very affectionately because she appeared to him as his mother. This incident forced him to confess to his psychotherapist after many years of this long-standing but extremely successfully hidden problem. Apparently in social situations he smiles in a friendly way at everybody, as he cannot discriminate between those whom he recognizes and those he does not.

Pseudocompetency is different from humility: whether true or false humility. It stems from the deep-rooted conviction: 'I haven't done what I know I can do.' To diagnose pseudocompetency accurately in ourselves we must have a sense of what the shortfall may be: those questions we are afraid the examiner, students or client may ask. We overperform or overachieve while knowingly or unconsciously hiding, covering up, faking or bluffing to minimize, obscure or avoid the particular gaps in our knowledge or skills. This is not done deliberately or even always consciously, but because the alternative is unthinkable. It is not deliberate deception, for example, 'I'm trying to be as honest as I can, but I still feel like a fraud', from a prestigious and politically sound professional in Bosnia who works himself into the ground until 2 or 3 am, covering the fact that he often feels a failure, can't handle personal relations and has no integration in the local community.

There is also a sense in which people particularly wanting survival in our society definitely benefit from pretending to know things that they do not know. For example, when taking a faulty car to the garage it is unwise for a woman to hand it over saying 'I don't know what is wrong with it – please just sort it out.' As Sally said: 'The bill could be enormous and you have no way of knowing if the work done was justified. If you can say you think it is the exhaust or the transmission, you know you are bluffing but feel you have made a stab at establishing your authority. If you don't bluff that you know what's what, you will be penalized for certain.'

Pseudocompetency also needs to be differentiated from the parent messages or 'driver behaviour' that can form a life script[4] for us. When parents originally give messages such as 'Be perfect', 'Hurry up', 'Be strong', 'Try hard' or 'Please me' then they, like Thetis, probably do so with the best of intentions. They want us to be excellent, fast, strong, brave and pleasing. It is only when these messages become linked conditionally with 'You're only OK if . . .' instead of being linked with our own stated goals that they become destructive. Then the child feels that their survival or their parents' love depends on how well they perform. These messages are sometimes misunderstood to mean that there is something wrong with a person's own aspirations to be fast, energetic, pleasing, strong or excellent. What distinguishes 'fast' from 'hurry' is that fast gets things done on time without feeling rushed. What distinguishes pleasing agreeableness from compulsive adaptation is that such pleasing is not compulsorily extended to everyone. Sometimes it is good to please people. What distinguishes trying hard (without success) from experimentation is that it does not demand that everyone try hard along with you. Being strong is partly about taking responsibility for your own needs, not about deliberately holding in your feelings or always keeping quiet. It is driven or compulsive behaviour if people believe that they have no other choice in different circumstances or with different people. However, the similarity between pseudocompetency and, for example, the driver behaviour is that people repeat the desire to achieve the scripted parental value (for example, to please), but they do so in a way guaranteed to fail again – just as it did originally.

How Does This Happen to People?

One of the reasons underlying this problem seems to be that there are often some grounds for the self-doubt – some truth – however small, in the feelings of faking it or anxiety. This puzzling discrepancy between externally perceived excellence and internally experienced inadequacy does indeed often cover an actual flaw or a developmental phase which the person skipped over. (Often this happened because teachers or parents thought that the individuals concerned were so talented that they would not need to learn such basic things or that they may be bored by them.) In this sense it is a 'normal' problem rather than a psychological abnormality. I want avoid pathologizing it, or making it seem like a sickness instead of an adaptation. Somethimes people suffer from their solutions.

Pseudocompetency means there is usually some authentic area in which the person is unsure because they had not mastered that aspect of their craft sufficiently or as thoroughly as perhaps less gifted people in that field. They may be conscious of it or not. The more technical name I have given the Achilles Syndrome is 'pseudocompetency'. It may not be the best term but it captures something of the (often unintentional) dishonesty involved in the work performance. It should never be used to put people down or insult them.

Pseudocompetent people *appear* competent and may be externally assessed to be very competent or even excellent. However their *inner* experience is the lack of confidence that they will be able to perform consistently well in their chosen field. They may or may not hide this self-doubt from their partner or friends. They can rarely perform without extremely severe anxiety hindering or even incapacitating them physically or psychologically in the long run. There is always the nagging fear of being shamed for a flaw which they have so far successfully hidden from others. Furthermore there is usually an unpleasant aftermath of extreme exhaustion. There is a kind of relief associated with escaping from a potentially very painful situation, rather than the glow of satisfaction which is the deserved outcome of a job well done.

For example, as a child I won an art prize, and was delighted, but knew that I did not really understand what I had done, or why it was good. I knew I'd be unlikely to repeat such a happy accident, since I knew nothing of drawing, colour, or painting techniques, and I was unwilling to master them. There was no knowledge of the in-between stages of learning. So I felt alienated from the product, unfamiliar with my own patterns of learning and skill-building, and untrusting of my own creative process. I slipped from not knowing how to paint to not knowing how I had painted so well. I had learned nothing to support me in painting in the future.

I have identified at least five major ways in which the syndrome of pseudocompetency is created and maintained. These are some preliminary answers to the questions, 'What are the causes?' and 'How does it happen?' The five reasons are: parental demands, childhood decisions about how to live life, educational mismanagement, collective forces and archetypal reasons. Each of these will be briefly discussed in turn and you will find further explanations throughout the rest of the book.

Many people grow up pseudocompetent because of unrealistic, punitive or manipulative parental demands. They may have to live up to very high expectations without being given the grounding or the necessary support. For example, Mohammed said despairingly: 'My mother expected me to be able to do anything whatsoever, and to do it perfectly.' Although on the one hand this can appear very positive, sometimes such expectations may not be appropriate or suited to the talents of the child, but they may have more to do with the wish-fulfilment of the parents, like Thetis, to have a brilliant, 'immortal' offspring. Sometimes a parent can coerce a child to try to make up by his or her achievements for the failures and disappointments of the parent's life.

Not only do parents place demands, wishes or manipulations on their children; *children themselves make decisions about how to live life*, or how to get on in the world. These decisions may or may not conform to what the parents impose upon them through threats, neglects, rewards or punishments. We have all had experiences of deciding never to do something again if we have been disappointed or shamed for showing excitement, vulnerability or even undisguised love. A little girl ran excitedly to her mother, saying 'I think Johnny loves me!' The mother turned on her with a sneer on her face, saying 'What makes you think that?' The little girl decided that she would never again trust her feelings about whether someone really liked her or not, since the mother's superior and hostile reaction was so damaging to her sense of trust in her own judgement in the field of human relationships.

These childhood decisions may form a kind of 'script' for their life which they then live out unless they rethink and change them. Other examples are people who decided as children that 'It is better to pretend that I understand than to be made to feel foolish when I ask a question' or 'I will conceal my regional accent because people laugh at my pronunciation.' We have all met people who bluff through speech patterns, taking on the accent or vocabulary of the type of person they would like to seem to others. Sometimes we discover the true accent or real voice – sometimes they reclaim their heritage, sometimes people can hide for ever.

Another important reason for the prevalence of the Achilles Syndrome are the *inadequacies, deficiencies, absurdities and cruelties of our educational systems*. Most people can recount many episodes where they have been let down, abused or exploited by teachers and others they looked up to for care and teaching. Sometimes important phases of learning are skipped over without a teacher noticing. Teachers may push bright children to perform for their own good reputation. We have read in the newspapers about gifted young gymnasts who win many prizes, heaping glory on their gym teachers or trainers but ending up with serious spinal injuries or eating disorders in the attempt to keep living up to the teacher's expectations. The ABCs of good health are not taken care of because the youngsters are so seduced by the teacher's attention on their pyrotechnic gymnastic displays, and the teachers are so seduced by the public attention.

Another pernicious cause of the large-scale pseudocompetence in our society is what can be described as *collective cultural forces*. This refers to the enormously subtle and pervasive influence in our culture on all of us, constantly exhorting us to be richer, thinner, younger, smarter, more 'sussed'. Some research has shown that we are exposed to more than 12,000 advertising messages in any given day. Most of these advertising messages encourage everybody to aspire to unrealistic ideals, and to feel bad if they do not live up to them. This is often unsupported by basic information about how to take care of oneself or a true assessment of the cost of the items. The popular, amusing and informative 'Bluff Your Way in . . .' handbooks on sale in even the most basic bookshops help create and support the conditions for pseudocompetency.

Deep inside our unconscious there are predisposing patterns, which may be personal patterns but are laid down by collective psychology, which guide us to recognize the shape of a story which we can adopt as our own. These are known as *archetypal patterns, images or predispositions*. The Achilles legend is one such archetype which seems to me to encompass most of the important aspects of this whole syndrome. All human beings search for stories or images from which we can learn and on which we can model ourselves and our lives. Old myths and legends, as much as the current heroes of stage and screen, provide us with such blueprints. The most important task is to recognize if we are learning from or trapped in archetypal patterns, and to find ways of becoming the authors of our own lives and our own stories.

The Fear of Being Found Out

As we have seen, the person with the Achilles Syndrome experiences a continual tension between the desire to do well and the desire to be helped in correcting or healing the flaw. This builds up into a vicious double-bind or 'Catch-22' situation where you lose either way.

As healthy human beings we want and need to get recognition and appreciation for our gifts. On the other hand, there is the nagging insecurity. This would find relief if we could persuade someone of the truth of our internal experience of incompetence in certain areas. Perhaps we can't get the help we desperately need or crave. Perhaps we are afraid to ask. But in asking for this kind of help at least two things may go wrong. Other people may disbelieve us and see us as weak or neurotic. At the other end of the scale, people may take us too seriously and over-react by taking our responsibility away or demoting us. Such an 'admission' or 'confession' may be used to penalize, humiliate, or injure our pride in the status we have enjoyed in our peer or employment group.

Admitting you do not think yourself truly competent (in all ways, in your field or in an organization), can be an act of self-destruction in an aggressive, macho-culture where performance is more important than future potential and the willingness to learn. 'The difficult thing in my life is defining myself as a consultant, it's like banging on a door saying "Open up, this is me, judge whether you would pay for it". I could market other things but when the product was me I couldn't. I can't bring myself to put out a marketing proposal; I keep tinkering with it but can't bring myself to publish it. I feel that it must be perfect before sending out a brochure.'

Dying of Shame

To be found out and exposed to all one's friends, acquaintances and enemies as having misled them on a vitally significant definition of one's self is experienced as mortifying.

Shame was very real for the Greek gods, as it remains for us today. Shame is one of the most excruciating of human emotions. When shamed one feels like 'falling into a hole in the ground'; wishes that one could be 'swallowed up by the earth'. There is always an element of wishing to disappear from view, of the desire not to be at the mercy of the other's shaming, accusing eyes. People will often use the expression 'I could have died for shame.' To be exposed to public view as having passed as an immortal when in fact he was only part-immortal could conceivably have been more humiliating to Achilles than death itself. We know that his proud mother felt diminished by being married to a mere mortal. Guilt is different from shame. We can feel *guilt* for some act of omission or commission we consider bad. Guilt has to do with behaviour for which we can apologize or atone. When we feel *shame* it is as if our whole *self* is bad. One client gave the following telling example:

'On my second day at school I wet my pants. No one had told me where the toilets were. I turned to the boy next to me and said, "What do you think that water is under my chair?" There was no shame about it. Then teacher pulled me out in front of the others, calling out "Come and wipe up!" The exposure was so shaming. Up till then it had been OK, it had been pleasant, warm.'

As a teenager May's mother tried to talk to her about menstruation. She was ashamed of it, and May became ashamed. Another woman had the opposite problem, of being treated as sexually mature before she was ready for it. Both spoke of a sense of silence in their shame and not being able to speak out. Shame stops us getting the information that would simply fix the problem.

Different cultures of course have different ways of educating, child-rearing and shaming. Certain religions have institutionalized shame. In some countries such as Britain I often find pseudocompetency is more prevalent among people who have greatly improved their life or education. It may be similar to someone from a working- or middle-class background suddenly appearing at a very smart dinner and not realizing that they are using the wrong fork, or cutting their bread instead of breaking it. They *know* that they deserve to be there because as people they are as worthwhile as anyone else. Yet, they may *feel* as if they don't really belong there. Subsequently, they may be too ashamed to admit to anyone that they don't know what to do, and so try and follow other people's example by watching and imitating in a surreptitious and tense way, all the while fearing that some perceptive person will notice their pretence, call their bluff, and announce to the whole table 'Anybody with any breeding would not hold a knife like a pencil!' In other countries parents may be so ashamed of only having girl babies that they choose to smother them at birth rather than endure the humiliation.

All human beings have deep psychological desires for immortality, invulnerability and irresistibility. We would like to live for ever, never be wounded and always be loved. Achilles' mother, Thetis, wanted him to be immortal too but did not quite succeed. Although he went into battle, had many victories, and achieved enormous personal power, he probably always had a sneaking fear that his secret vulnerability would be accidentally, maliciously, or fatally exposed. It is often easier to cover up a lie with another lie rather than face the embarrassment of admitting, not only the first bluff, but also the string of subsequent cover-ups. People overcompensate for their vulnerabilities and create a kind of armour around them. This armouring can be physical, where tension patterns become part of a body's very build and structure. Then this armour slows them down and draws attention to the very area they wish to hide. Examples are people with a thrust-forward jaw, chronically tensed-up shoulders, or an uptight backside. Body armouring is also closely linked with shame. 'I remember a school trip at 14, when teachers and pupils went nude bathing together. My friend said: "It's now or never." I took off my clothes and leapt in. I thought: "Shall I just die here in the water or come out and die of shame?"' If we spend too much time and energy being ashamed, embarrassed, cringing, sweaty and uptight, how little energy we will have left for learning.

People read these kinds of physical signals or body language from each other non-verbally all the time. A voice teacher[5] explained how monkeys indicate their status in the tribe by the way they walk about. The low-ranking monkeys shuffle about apologetically, shoulders hunched, eyes downcast, whimpering, quickly cowering out of the way of anyone who may have more right to the space, and giving very clear signals that, if anyone needed to be kicked or shoved, they were available victims. The macho young monkeys aspiring to become dominant in the tribe strut about with their jaws thrust forward, an aggressive cast to their eyes, threatening all and sundry with growls and menacing glances, their chests hugely inflated, legs wide apart. But the alpha monkey, the dominant one as the leader of the tribe, is much more relaxed than the others, striding about quite easily, cuffing gently here and there as necessary, but with an air of casual nonchalance. He is easy, sure of himself and of his competence. He appears to have nothing to prove. His confidence is matched by his competence.

Missing Out on the Basics

Theories of how children learn suggest that there are particular stages or critical periods which are ripe for the learning of certain skills. For example, certain language skills, if not acquired by age twelve, can only very rarely be learned after that age. If children pass by the critical developmental stage of acquiring a particular skill (while covering up) it can be extremely hard to return and pick up the ABCs. 'I feel as if I should, I feel as if *anybody* ought to be able to do it.' As studies have shown, for typists to increase their speed they actually have to slow down their typing speed first. When this happens they make many more mistakes and they feel much more clumsy before they get to the next stage of increased speed and improved accuracy. Another example is the very good table-tennis player who gets coaching for the first time and has to change the grip on the bat. At first this new style of play causes poorer performance and needs to be ridden through before 'excellence' can be achieved: 'It feels like I suddenly have to learn to write with my left hand when I am a right-hander.'

In taking on board new approaches to their work, counsellors may complain of being 'de-skilled'. We have to go through this period of conscious incompetence before we can become either consciously or unconsciously competent again. This is one of the important reasons people avoid going back to square one – because of the extremely uncomfortable, clumsy, insecure and unconfident self-perceptions which are associated in our culture with the early stages of learning. Although it is rare, you can even get to be a psychotherapist without having any personal therapy yourself – there are still some ways of training as a counsellor where nobody ever sees you actually work.

A brilliant young guitarist playing in several bands, with an excellent reputation both as player and improviser, cannot play the most elementary songs which many people start out with on the guitar. In itself this is no shame, but the young man *feels* that he is in some way a fraud in terms of his reputation as a brilliant guitarist. He avoids situations where this (to him) shameful secret may be exposed.

A professor of moral philosophy knows that he did not read a major section of basic philosophy, say logic, which is required study for all philosophy graduates. He has specialized and achieved international fame in an arcane branch of philosophy, but whenever he goes to a conference or a lecture he feels he will be found out. However, he keeps finding excuses for avoiding going back and letting colleagues know that he needs help in understanding the basic principles of logic which he skipped over in his undergraduate studies. The kind of discipline required to work through these problems in an undergraduate way is no longer an easy part of his 'intellectual muscle'. He is embarrassed to ask for help, reluctant to do the exercises, feels he does not have the time it will take to plug this gap in his expertise. Yet he keeps fearing that one day he will be embarrassingly exposed and shamed. Frequently, true competency involves being competent enough to be willing to go back and learn the basics again, to allow others, even your juniors, to teach you. It requires a willingness to experience the state of beginning again – sometimes even to tolerate feeling slow, clumsy and hesitant again – to be like the baby learning to walk. Babies are usually not afraid to try, to fail, to try again and again until they achieve mastery.

In Western culture there is unfortunately much shame attached to learning and to being a beginner. 'Greenhorns' are the butt of many jokes and, as we will see later, knowledge is also closely linked with shame. Curing pseudocompetency usually entails scrupulous honesty with oneself. Some of the discrepancy and harshness of self-judgement may well be unjust and unfair, but if someone is truly competent in their field, they also have a very good sense of the parts of their discipline which they skipped over, or where they took it easy, avoided learning 'the hard stuff' and so on. There is therefore usually a grain of truth in the subjective 'negative' assessment. People with this problem tend to avoid or postpone situations where they will be tested and they have a low frustration tolerance threshold – they have difficulty in putting up with the inevitable stops and starts, progressions and regressions, of the learning process.

When I have put out publicity for workshops on the Achilles Syndrome, I have often received letters saying 'I am surprised to find myself running a large organization' or 'I find myself earning a lot of money.' The honesty in the way the writers have expressed themselves shows that something being covered up is causing unnecessary strain on people. The Achilles Syndrome is not a tight stultifying term meant to 'box', categorize or insult people, as we saw in the preface. Some people have found it a useful name given to a set of problems which hinder people in their well-being, their development and in celebrating their capacities, skills and talents. It is phenomenological in a descriptive and existential sense; that is, it can only be truly felt by the individual, 'inside'. We will recognize it in others or ourselves, and if the identification of the problem helps us resolve it, the terminology serves its purpose. There are also, of course, many fluctuations in the way we feel about our competencies over time, and in different people we will find many gradations of the problem. Some have a fully developed Achilles Syndrome affecting their entire personality, outlook on life and destiny; for others it affects smaller areas of their lives, or only during certain times. For most people there are probably some aspects of their ability, talent, or attractiveness which they feel they are faking in the way which is here being described as pseudocompetency.

Suggestions and Exercises

- Make a list of the activities or qualities about which you have fooled people successfully for many years.
- Write down a dream which you remember about performance anxiety.
- Using the chart below, make a list of competencies. 'I know how to do this, and other people know I know how to do this.'
- Make a list of incompetencies you would like to change.
- Make a list of incompetencies you don't mind about. This brings its own freedom.
- In an area in which people consider you to be experienced, differentiate between what you really know and where you may have twenty years' experience of covering up the same mistakes.
- Decide what field of competency you are most concerned about and then define the criteria for what you would consider to be 'good enough' for you in that field.

- Make a list of occasions where you messed up, had accidents or made mistakes. What were you trying to communicate to your significant others at that time?
- Make a list of things you would like to be able to do by the end of the year and then write alongside them what you

need to do in order to be able to do them by the end of the
year.
• What were your reactions to doing these first exercises?

IDENTIFY YOUR:

Competencies
Incompetencies you would like to change
Incompetencies you don't mind
Areas of pseudocompetency

CHAPTER TWO

Recognizing Achilles

HOW TO RECOGNIZE ACHILLES – THE IDENTIFYING CHARACTERISTICS IN ONESELF AND OTHERS

Priam let his eyes dwell on Achilles and saw with admiration how big and beautiful he was, the very image of a god. (p. 454) Achilles sprang to meet him. . . . . He kept his front covered with his decorated shield. (p. 405)

This chapter deals with how to recognize pseudocompetency in oneself and others and discusses the identifying characteristics in depth, along with the other problems that frequently accompany this syndrome.

Recognizing the Achilles Syndrome

I have found that pseudocompetency can affect anybody, from the housewife who builds up a reputation for excellent dinner parties but who makes herself sick with worry before each one, to the internationally acclaimed barrister who breaks out in a cold sweat at the very thought of representing a client in court. No matter how big the fee or how successful the newspaper reports, he/she feels that he/she is somehow either a failure or a fraud. Another woman enjoys planning her parties but never feels truly satisfied when they are over. They leave her with a huge let-down feeling afterwards: 'While it's going on, it's glorious. Then everyone goes home and I am left – and feeling a sick-child feeling inside'.

There are examples of pseudocompetency from all walks of life, such as the financial genius who manipulates a fortune of billions, always *fearing* that one day it will go wrong (as it sometimes does). As he gets to such a senior position no one dares confront him any more, and perhaps no one tried to help until it was too late. We frequently read in the news-papers about such people who finally 'crash' spectacularly, and perhaps commit suicide. Then people find out what they had been covering up for a long time: for example, huge amounts missing from a corporate pension fund.

It also applies to the professor with a PhD in psychology who does not know her multiplication tables. She therefore does not really understand the implications of psychological research and so lectures her students on statistics in a state of nerves. She dreads the day some bright student may catch her out in this area of incompetence, so carefully hidden behind the veneer of a brilliant all-round academic awarded prizes for her contribution to the field. There is also, for example, the secretary who can't spell because she's dyslexic or was often ill at school. She spends tea breaks and lunchtimes frantically looking up words. The spellchecker on her word-processor works overtime, often at some cost to her overall efficiency. Even when she makes the grade, she is tense, irritable and worried. Her greatest anxiety is that someone will one day uncover the secret that she really cannot spell and expose her to the shame of colleagues and bosses who believed better of her. Her *reputation* as an efficient, supercompetent secretary is thus maintained, but at the cost of great tension, interpersonal impoverishment and a daily drainage of self-esteem in the face of much external appreciation.

Although people can experience the Achilles Syndrome in very different ways, as shown in Chapter 1, I have identified the following seven features which people report most commonly:

1. a mismatch between externally assessed competence or qualification and internally experienced competence or capability, leading to feelings of 'I'm a fraud';
2. inappropriate anxiety or panic in anticipation of doing the relevant task;
3. inappropriate strain or exhaustion after the task;
4. relief instead of satisfaction on completion of a task;
5. inability to carry over any sense of achievement to the next situation;
6. a recurrent conscious or unconscious fear of being found out, and of shame and humiliation;
7. a longing to tell others about the discomfort but the fear of being called weak or unstable. This sense of a taboo adds to the strain, loneliness and discomfort.

We will now look at each of these features of the Achilles Syndrome in turn.

Discrepancy Between Externally Assessed Competence and Internally Experienced Competence

As we have seen, this mismatch between others' opinion of us and our own is at the heart of the Achilles Syndrome. For example, researchers recently asked men and women about their fluency in a foreign language. Men would class themselves as 'fluent' with an O-level in French. Women with honours degrees in modern languages would call themselves only 'rusty' or 'fairly fluent'. The subjectivity of the judgement of internally experienced competence is what makes the problem difficult to handle, and what leads to the person's feeling of being misjudged by others.

A very able and popular woman told me about her job:

I still felt like the youngest in the class, that I couldn't get too close to any of the team because if they really saw then they'd find out. I used to keep myself on the fringe but I looked like a central person in that job. I was popular and people wanted to be with me, like an attractive bee. But there would be a moment

when I would skirt away from them. I used to get very frightened that, if they stayed around me long enough, they would
find me out.

Inappropriate Anxiety or Panic in Anticipation of Doing the Relevant Task

It is characteristic that pseudocompetent people keep looking for a cure, a teacher, a guru, another course, qualification,
or challenge. They may be hoping all the while that, somewhere, someone will help them identify those gaps and help
them to fill them. It would be vital to do this without them
having to 'lose face' or be shamed in the very way that they
were shamed when the roots of the problem were first laid
down. Of course what it leads to is an inhibition in pleasure
of performance; a lack of joy in the work; an eventual dread
of the work.

A trainee counsellor told me:

> I started as a musician. I'd be sick on the way to performances.
> I don't know how I got my music diplomas. I did get through,
> but it was horrific. My mind went blank and my hands shook. I
> changed a lot when I did the counselling diploma exam.
> I approached it differently, put to rest some of the old ghosts. I
> used to be surprised when what I did worked. I used to feel it
> was luck.

People with the Achilles Syndrome may over-prepare for a
task, based on the fear and belief 'If I don't, they will catch
me out.' In this way they panic the night before, read dozens
of books to prepare for a half-hour lecture and frighten
themselves sick out of fear that someone will ask them a
question they will be unable to answer.

People are not frightened in the areas of their competence. They look forward to doing the task, enjoy doing it
and feel joy and satisfaction afterwards. Preparation is a
whole-person experience, involving excitement and comfort in one's body, and supported by one's fantasies and
dreams. But if people have never had the experience of true

competency, it may be impossible for them to conceive of anything in the future but a repeat of the painful experience of pseudocompetency.

Inappropriate Strain or Exhaustion After the Task

Many people complain of coming away exhausted, burnt out or drained after performing in their personal areas of pseudocompetency. I have been told that the Achilles Syndrome workshops can also bring out great strain and fatigue for participants at the end of each day; 'simply from facing up to the truth'. It is naturally tiring to live in a state of fear, tension and internal chaos around our work – a major source of self-esteem and recognition in our culture.

In curing pseudocompetency we have to keep reviewing the appropriateness of our fatigue. It's fine to be tired after we've done something difficult, but the Achilles Syndrome throws out this natural balance. Being tired for a long time may signal that this exhaustion is inappropriate to that energy expenditure. We each have to assess the appropriate level for ourselves, just as pseudocompetency is not something with which you can label other people. It's something that people can recognize for themselves – and only they can really know. It's not something that can be objectively judged by others. You know for yourself the difference between feeling tired from a good run or job well done, and the bone-weary fatigue from having avoided 'being found out' too much, too long.

Relief Instead of Satisfaction on Completion of a Task

It is natural to feel satisfied on completing a task, to review the job and feel pleasure at the parts done well and to clarify and learn what could still be improved or done differently. The Achilles Syndrome and its build-up of tension robs us of this true satisfaction exactly because we feel we are frauds.

Any relief we feel is because there was so much at stake, not because we feel we did well. 'I only thank God I got away with it again.'

There is no genuine satisfaction or pleasure. The short-lived relief will also at times turn into dread of the next task. The relief does not feel genuinely earned and therefore cannot add to (it may even detract from) our self-esteem. A well-regarded and seemingly able and competent worker told me:

> I can't even feel relief any more each time I get through a job. I get superstitious about my competence. I feel that if I let myself know that something has gone well, it will go wrong. Pride brings about a fall. It hangs over me like the sword of Damocles. I can be very confident and know my area well, and then suddenly something can throw me. Now I'm dealing with this injury that could have demolished me.

Inability to Carry Over Any Sense of Achievement to the Next Situation

Another identifying characteristic of people with the Achilles Syndrome is that they don't believe that the victory of one occasion carries over to the next. Instead of feeling satisfied and happy that they have, for example, made a good public speech, they tell themselves that it was a fluke, that they were just lucky, that it was an easy audience (or an easy exam). The abilities displayed do not increase or enhance the person's self-confidence in facing another task of a similar level of challenge. External observers may describe such a response as false modesty, but I am suggesting this must be taken very seriously. It is usually an expression of someone's genuine self-assessment, although the content may be inaccurate (for example, perhaps it *was* a good speech or an easy audience). We owe it to ourselves and others to identify, confront and resolve this limitation to actualization and reaching and fulfilling our potentials as people and as professionals. Pseudocompetents are overcontrolled in areas where they shouldn't be, and yet also undercontrolled in areas where they shouldn't be. They also often complain of feeling that they do not belong to any group, for they do not feel genuinely themselves. It is a matter of being true to yourself and at the same time being naturally ambitious to get yourself where you want to be.

Tony, the nervous public speaker, found this helpful. He discovered that he could gain a sense of achievement by being very clear about the subject areas he was truly competent to speak about. Once he had done this he found he knew what to do next:

> I under-controlled the publicity – what I am billed to speak on – and how it relates to what I am going to say and what the audience is prepared to hear from me. I have learned after several mistakes that I need to check the publicity very carefully indeed and get the right context for me to be and feel competent as well as confident.

Recurrent Conscious or Unconscious Fear, Shame, Humiliation, of Being Found Out

Faked orgasms, the see-saw pseudo-control of bulimia, the brittle aggressiveness of a personality who hasn't learnt how to stand up for itself in a genuinely assertive way – all these are possible indicators of pseudocompetency in otherwise competent individuals. These are often the people who excel but always feel vulnerable because they are sure that, somehow, somebody, someday is going to find and expose their fatal flaw. Thus, even though they may appear to have a lot of self-confidence, they often spend their lives covering up – the pseudocompetent person is very aware of that specific flaw. They fear having it flayed open and displayed against the background of their previously achieved excellence. That would be the excruciating feared humiliation which people will go to great lengths to avoid. In this way they keep trying to put off the shaming exposure. Their fear is always that others will 'find them out' or 'see through them' because deep down they are whispering to themselves: 'I know about the missing bits. My sense of the aesthetic, the truth, is disturbed by it.' People may have recurrent nightmares or dreams of being in public places without their clothes, being discovered and laughed at. These may have individual meanings, but Achilles would recognize the dread involved.

Longing to Talk About the Discomfort but the Fear of Being Called Weak or Unstable

As pseudocompetency continues, the effort of maintaining the façade seems to become greater, draining people's energy, confidence and self-esteem still further. When a point of sufficient desperation is reached, people will be covering up and yet starting to drop hints at the same time, caught in a vicious circle of experiencing the symptom and suppressing it, so they transmit the double message: 'Find me out/Don't find me out.' The 'find me out' message is the weaker one because of the strength of the cover-up; yet the simultaneous brittleness of the cover-up could be shattered in one go by being found out.

The following example shows the child's desperation to break the cycle by telling the truth:

> My mother had very high expectations of me and I took on that role. I had to provide that for her, keeping her happy, safe and content. No matter what price I had to pay. So, if I felt very scared (and I felt scared a lot, and sad), the one thing I knew absolutely in my bones that I couldn't do was tell her, because I was meant to provide the security and the parenting for her. I do remember sometimes crying because I couldn't hold back my tears and all she would do then was cry too, and I'd need to strengthen up and get on with really providing her with the service that she wanted. I was thinking it was never OK for me to be ordinary and so I felt insecure saying just ordinary childish things.

Feelings of fraudulence often stem from acting as other people expect us to be. On looking back to the roots of her pseudocompetency problem, Megan saw that she did not want to change her fundamental nature, but instead her attitudes and reactions to others and herself:

> I don't want to throw out the qualities that I did have then. It's an acceptance of that part of me that's been very important. Even now I think I was probably a wise kid. I probably did have qualities that really got me through and if that was interpreted by them as an old head on young shoulders, that's their interpretation. I don't agree with their interpretation but I agree for myself that I was a tenacious kid.

Why is the Achilles Syndrome so Important?

The cost in terms of human pain and suffering of children, workers, executives, public performers, parents and gifted individuals in a great many disciplines is enormous. I have come across so many people in various fields of human endeavour who feel great relief and understanding when they have heard the material on pseudocompetency. Instead of feeling ashamed or insulted they feel curious, understood and helped. 'I realize it has affected my confidence, my pleasure in my work, my authority as a teacher in consistently negative and undermining ways. This realization alone has already reduced my anxiety.'

People often report that they use drugs, alcohol or sexual promiscuity to overcompensate for the deep and abiding fear of letting slip the secret covered-up inadequacy behind the glittering and super-confident façade. Some students commit suicide because of a fear of losing their track record of all 'A's. The flaw is the belief that 'I'm only OK if I'm perfect.' They became mortally terrified of examinations or other testing situations where their incompetencies or hidden areas of ignorance may be fatefully exposed. They would just not know what to do if they failed. The fear of their parents' and teachers' disappointment if they appeared less than adequate is so overwhelming that they would sometimes rather die than risk exposure of their vulnerable 'heel' in the battle of examination or competition. It is brave to decide to learn a new thing, to expose the 'nakedness' of oneself 'not-knowing'.

Why is it so Often Overlooked?

Perhaps a reason for the fact that this problem is so often overlooked is that so many of the judges or external assessors themselves suffer from the Achilles Syndrome. They too may be 'covering up' in fear some fundamental ignorance or incompetence which, if exposed, would be mortifyingly shameful and disappointing to everyone who believed in them, praised them, and gave them their 'superior status'. These are the individual reasons for fighting against acknowledging it in oneself, which brings the difficulty in recognizing and identifying it in others.

It is as if we have become a society where we collude with each other in 'covering up' our fatal flaws because we are ashamed to have them publicly exposed. Unfortunately, the more we collude in this mutual pretence, the more excruciating the tension of maintaining the secret becomes. There are thus individual and collective reasons for avoiding acknowledgement of this problem, for continuing to deny its existence and overlooking the enormous costs of maintaining the façade. This is unfortunate because there is indeed hope and fulfilment possible if people can but begin to recognize this syndrome and start resolving it.

As I pointed out at the beginning, it is a basic motivation of children and developing adults to want to be competent. Learning a new skill or new knowledge brings its own challenges, but particularly its own rewards. Pseudocompetent people, however, want to go from incompetence to competence without any of the in-between stages. As a student said to me once, only half-joking: 'God forbid anyone should see me learning!' They frequently want to avoid ever feeling incompetent, de-skilled or clumsy again. For true learning to take place, this is an impossible desire. Feeling and behaving incompetently seems to be always a necessary stage in learning new skills or new knowledge. Unfortunately, our society and teachers have often made us feel that this part of the learning process – conscious incompetency – is shameful. There is a collective pressure in our society to cover up the fatal flaw. Teachers may collude with us, partly because they do not want their own incompetencies and concomitant lies to be exposed, partly because they would not know what to do if they were.

Suggestions and Exercises

- Make a list of things you would say you are incompetent about, but your colleagues would say you are competent about.
- What are you afraid that people will find out about you that you can't do or don't know?
- Write some publicity material for yourself. Who does it seem to be aimed at? Is it the right context?
- Identify the strain or shaming trauma that led to the cover-up. (If you live in a family which does not value you as a person or in an atmosphere in which everyone is a high achiever, the effect is of strain (cumulative) rather than trauma (one-off).)
- What is your memory of the most shaming incident in your life and how could it be done differently now? How could the shamer's words or actions have been different? How could your own response have been different?
- Shame – is there something you can identify as being ashamed about, or having been shamed? Are you ready to let go of it now?
- What is the most vicious and destructive criticism you have ever received? How can you stop yourself being affected by that, or ever letting yourself be hurt by that again?

CHAPTER THREE

The Childhood of Achilles

UNDERSTANDING PSEUDOCOMPETENCY IN ITS CHILDHOOD ROOTS

Achilles wept. He sat down by himself on the shore of the grey sea, and looked across the watery wilderness. Then, stretching out his arms, he poured out prayers to his Mother. 'Mother, since you, a goddess, gave me life, if only for a little while, surely Olympian Zeus the Thunderer owes me some measure of regard. But he pays me none.' (p. 32)

This chapter explores the childhood roots of pseudocompetency, bringing together new child development studies emphasizing children's need for mastery, competence, and meaning-making, and how this is connected with our sense of ourselves as autonomous agents – authors of our own lives. The parental and societal manipulation and distortion of these needs of the child and the damaging and destructive effects of shaming and humiliation will be explored. Shame will be differentiated from guilt, and guilt is also discussed.

General Child Development Theory

Counselling and psychotherapy have often in the past focused on inborn sexual and aggressive drives which are mostly unconscious. On the other hand some psychologists have modelled their theories on animals, tending to view people as reactive to their environment – learning like rats through conditioning, as a result of what their environment rewards or punishes. In the behaviourist model of human functioning, competency became associated with the idea that we become effective or successful in response to this reward or punishment. In the psychoanalytic model, creativity and competence were usually associated with sublimation or perversion of sexual and aggressive drives. Until quite recently, child development theory tended to focus on how a child developed into a mature sexual being. The child's need for love was acknowledged, but its need for mastery, competence and the creation of meaning as acts of initiative by which the child shapes its world was largely neglected.

In the clinical and academic environment in which most mental-health professionals train, there have been a number of very important challenges in the last decade or so to the established views of child development and human motivation. There is now a great deal more writing on the child's development of competency and the mastery of skills and tasks. However strange this may seem to the layperson who has watched real children grow and learn, the basic drive of human beings for competency, creativity and evolution is just beginning to be acknowledged in the mainstream psychological literature.

The Desire to Know

It seems astonishing to me that it is only comparatively recently that the idea of competence as an important drive, observable in human babies, has emerged. More and more researchers and professional people observing infants are recognizing and validating what many parents know and many children strive for – the motivation and pleasure in being efficient or competent. Other researchers on infants have now noticed that infants begin to smile when they have a sense that they can affect the external world in an effective or competent way. One of the central issues in this book is that human life is not only about survival or death but also about the pleasure and joy in being competent.

One of the most important findings of modern child development theory is that the infant has a *self* much earlier than previously believed; a self which is very active in creating meaning and organization. Our sense of self is strengthened and nourished when we succeed in doing something we want or when we achieve mastery or competence in a particular task or learn how to do something difficult. The child actually enjoys and needs to become competent at many life tasks – from tying shoelaces to making a new friend. It is therefore natural to human nature to get pleasure from gaining knowledge, just as it is natural to seek intimate relationships.

This drive for learning and creative expression can be referred to as Physis or the 'élan vital' – the vital energy of life itself. The Greek philosophers were talking about Physis thousands of years ago in the following way:

> Nature, or Physis . . . shapes the seed into a tree or the blind puppy into a good hound. The perfection of the tree or the blind puppy is in itself indifferent, a thing of no ultimate value. Yet the goodness of Nature lies in working for that perfection.[1]

When the Desire to Know Goes Wrong

However, somehow in our collective consciousness, having or seeking knowledge is connected with shame, and thus also with sexuality. A writer found it difficult to give her parents the copy of her latest book that they expected so eagerly and proudly, because she knew she had written honestly in it about her childhood misunderstandings of sex and love. She resorted to slicing out the particular pages that might be hurtful to them, hoping that they would not notice the gaps in the page numbering.

Psychoanalysis can tend to regard this thirst for knowledge as an extension of sexual curiosity or as a sublimation of oral drives. Psychoanalytic writings also maintain that there is a close link between sadism and the desire to know. Sartre pointed out that having, doing and being are the three main categories of human reality, and that knowing is a modality of having. The powerful Bible image of the fall from Eden underlines the perceived danger of having knowledge:

> And when the woman saw that the tree was good for food, and that it was pleasant to the eyes, and a tree to be desired to make one wise, she took of the fruit thereof, and did eat, and gave also unto her husband with her; and he did eat. And the eyes of both of them were opened, and they knew that they were naked; and they sewed fig leaves together and made themselves aprons. . . . And unto Adam he said: 'Cursed is the ground for they sake; in sorrow shalt thou eat of it all the days of they life . . . the man is become as one of us, to know good and evil.'[2]

The following story illustrates how a natural desire to know became a pseudocompetency problem in one young boy named Teddy:

> At nursery school one day the clock in the classroom stopped. The teacher asked me to go to the hall to find out the time as I was one of the few in the class who could tell the time. I ran out to the hall quite eagerly and stared at the clock above the window. I stared for a long time. I was horrified to discover I could make no sense of the clock. It was round and had two hands like any other clock. But it had, to me, no recognizable numbers. They were Roman numerals. To me they were an unknown language, a confusion of 'I's, 'X's and 'V's that seemed to crowd around the edge of the clock in random fashion. They made no sense at all.
>
> Looking back from this vantage point four decades later, I wonder what would have happened if I had simply returned to the class and admitted I didn't understand the clock. In the event, I was too terrified to return with such a confession. After all, I was meant to know, I was expected to know. I had been specially chosen for this mission, being one who could tell the time. I felt such deep shame at the knowledge that I could not fulfil what was expected of me, so much so that I panicked. I ran back to the classroom and on entering cried out: 'I can't find the clock!' which, of course, was greeted with more derisive laughter than if I had simply told the truth. The teacher, with a look

of disgust at me, chose another pupil to fulfil the task – someone, she said, who was a bit more observant. I returned to my seat crest-fallen but my secret inadequacy was safe.

It was many years before I got to grips with Roman numerals. In the meantime, I learned to get by when faced with a clock with Roman figures by approximating the position of the Arabic equivalents. Approximating was a skill that covered much ignorance in my childhood. I learned to externally appear confident and knowledgeable while internally I was experiencing the same shame and terror I had experienced as I stared at the clock in the school hall.

Teddy was incompetent at reading Roman numerals at the time his teacher asked him to check the time on the school clock. He *was* competent at reading the time on any clock with Arabic numerals. Pseudocompetency arose because there was an area of learning which his teacher thought he had accomplished but which he had not, in fact, mastered. He was too ashamed to tell her this, choosing rather to risk her anger than to 'lose face' by admitting what he did not know.

The Role of Shame in Shaping the Achilles Syndrome

Shame can be a very debilitating childhood trauma that continues to have a deep effect upon our adult lives. The vividness of the examples proves how alive the traumatic experience remains within us as adults decades later:

> The shame I experienced when I did my 11-plus exam! I didn't get straight through, I needed to take an oral exam as well. I didn't get through to the school my mother wanted me to go to. She'd already bought the blazer. I went to a technical high school, but I felt terrible because I hadn't come up to my mother's expectations. The shame . . . for four years my mother tried to get me into the other school. Eventually there was a place – I refused then because I was happy where I was. But I felt shame.

This story illustrates a child's natural drive to protect its own organismic integrity in whatever way it can with the limited resources available to it.

At home I was taught to play the piano and was rapped on the knuckles when I got it wrong. The exam was coming up but I couldn't pull myself together so my mother got me some Valium from the doctor. This happened for a few years and I continually asked to stop. I finally threw up on the piano. Then I could blame it on a physical illness so that I could stop. And my mother felt the shame of that – I've always been proud of that! The teacher said he could hear a beautiful sound suddenly stop. That was when I vomited on the piano.

Another example of the child Achilles growing to the adult comes from the psychotherapist who told her client: 'You never let people see you knowing nothing or in the process of learning – you've got to go from crawling to being a perfect runner.' He replied with a sudden flash of insight: 'I never did crawl.' He understood that, by a kind of stripping process, you have to get back to being the baby who doesn't know what to do at all. Then you try things, make mistakes and try again; and if necessary you let someone else in on your learning process. So often what happens in this kind of case is the same symbolically as going from lying in your cot straight into walking: being deprived of all the middle stages of the learning cycle. And later we will not feel really solid on our feet because we missed out the developmental phase and didn't develop the neurological movements and pathways to support that. It happens both psychologically and physically:

As a child I was often treated by my parents as a pseudo-adult. I was flattered but realized later I had lost out on the chance to play and just be silly. I was always having to achieve. I felt the tyranny of their praise. Afterwards it is a terrible thing to admit that you are just ordinary in many ways.

A major feature of the addiction of appearing competent and avoiding learning or being seen to be learning is that you may either find or seek out teachers who themselves don't know or can't admit that they don't know things or even where to find them out. If a child asks for an explanation the teacher can either give it, say 'Go and look it up' or send him away. The child may never learn that knowing where and how to find it out is as important or more important than knowing. They may learn only ways of keeping themselves in the trap:

> I was the youngest of a very big family. I had three brothers and tried to be equal. At family mealtimes I used to have to rush to get my share, then to get my second helping just like all the others. It represents a lot about me trying to keep up all my life. Any achievement had always been done before, so I had to rush on to the next thing.

Children who have the opportunity of assimilating learning before moving on are able to resist the onset of the Achilles Syndrome so much better than their less fortunate brothers and sisters. This phase of assimilation will vary according to each child's individual temperament.

I find in teaching that the four human temperament types are easiest to understand in diagram form. The nature of our temperaments would look like Figure 3.1 in wave form.

Your temperament is what works for you. We may be fast or slow, strong or gentle. If you are not sure what temperamental type you are, one way of working this out is to consider the question: Do you primarily relate to life in terms of the past, the present, or the future, or a combination of these three?

1. *Intuitive* types: relate to reality through awareness and anticipation of the future.
2. *Sensation* types: focused on the present, they are involved with what is happening around them and within them now.
3. *Feeling* types: relate to the past, they are interested in how things used to be, they carry a historical awareness and a sense of tradition.
4. *Thinking* types: go from the past to the present to the future, walking a logical line between them; they are the most highly rewarded in our culture.

Fast &
Strong

Slow &
Strong

Fast &
Gentle

Slow &
Gentle

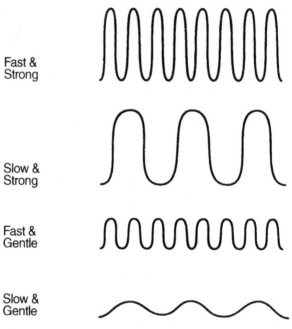

Figure 3.1. The Four Temperaments in Wave Form

The Child Achilles

Great Expectations

Sometimes looking at the mythological story can give us some ideas of the important components in the formation of this particular problem. The story of Achilles is long and complex but I will highlight three features which seem relevant to the understanding of the origins as well as the therapy of this syndrome. These are good expectations, early success, and training in pretence. As we have seen in the first chapter, Achilles' mother Thetis was very ambitious for him, dipping him in the Styx – the river of death – so that he would become an immortal. This was the status she had longed for but was unable to achieve, so she appears to have transferred this ambition onto her son with perilous consequences.

In fact, some stories say that the six brothers of Achilles had perished before from the ambitious actions of their mother to make them immortal. It is only because his father snatched him from the fire that he survived at all. Clinically I have frequently found that people who suffer from pseudo-competency have been pressurized by their parents, often by an ambitious mother who did not achieve her own potential, to become high achievers (and make her proud) at some cost to their own well-being.

Early Success

As you will remember, Thetis really wanted to marry a god and felt she had 'come down' in the world in being the wife of the mortal Peleus. When she deserted her husband, Peleus took Achilles to be tutored by 'the civilized centaur' Chiron, who gave him special food such as the marrow of bears to give him courage and the marrow of fawns to give him swiftness. He sounds like the modern youngster on vitamins who goes from dancing to art classes, to piano lessons, to scout meetings, to the tennis club. In the story Achilles learned running, hunting, pipe playing, healing and singing at banquets. He was very, very talented; at the age of six he had already killed his first boar! He attracted the admiration of the gods for his speed, agility and hunting prowess.

In a similar way, many modern Achilles have early successes. Often these are so impressive that both parents and teachers are blinded to the developmental or emotional needs of these youngsters. The premature successes become an emotional burden because the young person feels that they may never be able to pull it off again, since they don't quite understand in a considered and integrated way how it happened that they had such success so quickly, and why the grown-ups are applauding their achievements instead of trying to help the youngster cope with them.

Training in Pretence

It had been foretold that Troy could not be conquered without the aid of Achilles, who would die in the war. So Thetis, again from the good motivation to protect him, dressed him as a girl and sent him to live in the palace of another king where he lived under an assumed name. When Odysseus, Nestor and Ajax – Greek warlords – came to fetch Achilles, they could not find him in their search through the palace. However, the shrewd and wily Odysseus laid a trap for him. He brought presents for the women of the court; beautiful jewels, girdles, dresses and cloaks – but he included a shield and spear. The charade of Achilles as a girl in the king's court continued until a call to arms was sounded. Odysseus had ordered a trumpet call to war to trick Achilles out of his disguise. The ruse worked because when Achilles heard the sound of impending battle he took off his girls' clothes and ran to take up the shield and spear. Having been thus discovered, Achilles had little choice but to lead his troops towards his fated death on the bloody battlefields of Troy.

Modern young Achilles often have similar stories in their childhood. Even though they may be less dramatic, they may be no less painful. I have often been told of children (who suffer eventually from pseudocompetency) being dressed in the apparel of the opposite sex, being asked to lie on behalf of the parents to rent collectors or family, or engaging in some form of subterfuge, including attending schools which would not under other circumstances have accepted them.

Being and Doing

Children who are praised for doing rather than being are particularly prone to pseudocompetency in later life, feeling perhaps that they will not be loved or valued unless they pass their exams. It can turn into a superstition:

> I had a false belief about exams that if I said I failed, then I passed. I really believed this, and also that if I told Mum I'd

failed then I'd passed. If I did pass then it would be a surprise, and so I always used to do the same thing in tests – I had tricked myself but also I was doing it because actually I did not know what was expected.

In fact pseudocompetents' judgement is very faulty so they don't know when they've done good work or bad work. They'd come out of an exam and not be able to tell you whether they did well or badly. Whereas the competent kids come out of the exam and can give you an estimate of how well they did.

However, children who are praised for being rather than doing have their own set of pseudocompetency problems. People who are appreciated only for being do not learn to have conditional strokes. When they enter systems such as education or work, they are shocked that people should be conditional with them. Both polarities suffer from the tyranny of praise:

> As an adult I went on a crash course to learn French. We were all sitting there blushing at the fear of getting a word wrong. The internal critics were getting in too soon on the learning process. In our culture, there is so much shame attached to this.

The domains of being and of doing are easy to confuse. To be valued for being ('I like you for what you are') is very different from being valued for doing ('I like you for what you produce, for the way you perform in the world'). A very angry disabled man recently spoke out about a current trend to romanticize or idealize the situation of the disabled, by quoting their achievements in athletics or breaking records – when in fact most disabled people's lives are simply not like that and the vast majority are engaged in the task of coping with their own everyday life. This brings with it the danger of jumping to the opposite conclusion – thinking that the answer is therefore not to value the disabled record-breakers. This is also a confusion in the domains of being and doing. What people are is not the same as what people do, and all human beings deserve to be valued for both. It is extremely hard for people in our society to separate these two out. The woman in an earlier example who was left feeling badly let down after her dinner parties came to see that: 'Afterwards I realized how much I didn't get for my being – I got the praise for my doing.' In this culture, we can become so desperate to get our strokes for doing that we completely 'forget' or overlook the value of the opposite pole, of being. Achilles was valued for what he could *do*, not what he *felt*.

To value someone for being is to grant them unconditional acceptance and value as a person. If a person does not have basic affirmation of the worth of their own being, or in extreme cases if they feel for various reasons that they do not deserve even to exist at all, then their fundamental self is under threat – they can't *do* very much. Counsellors and therapists are trained not to do in-depth work on pseudo-competency issues when their client is in trauma, pain, or rage. If someone is trying to be competent when their very organism (their very being) is under threat, then that is highly dangerous. As a recent trainee on an Achilles workshop put it:

> If I am performing in the world, and others say it's all OK but I am not feeling that, then those are the strokes I only get for doing, providing or producing. Our collective cultural conditioning is that we have to *do* in order to *be*. We need to give ourselves permission to exist whether or not we perform.

It is a natural life force to want to perfect yourself, or to grow and evolve, but there is no value system to say that a lion is 'better' than a tree, or a giraffe is less important than a rat. An ancient Greek philosopher used the example of a blind puppy who wants to achieve the best that a blind puppy can achieve. We can see this desire for competence and mastery in children and animals – how they like to show off before they are damaged by the tragic loss of moving from 'Look Mummy!' to 'I can't do it, I'm embarrassed.' Working dogs are happy to show off what they know. Sometimes circus animals are harmed both by cruel punishment and when they are rewarded for doing things injurious or unnatural to them. This is a perversion of that natural drive for mastery. Humankind is the only species that has perverted this drive. However, it is not the drive for excellence that is the problem, or what people want to achieve, but how it gets manipulated by people through punishment/reward systems. In a culture that values achievement and rewards it, how can we not devalue the failures or the ordinary, the average, the good enough?

We need to be strong in the value statements that we live and make, when faced with strong collective pressures. Exams are to test people's *doing*, not being. Our leadership figures need to keep teaching this. Even if mistakes are made, we still have permission to exist. Even murderers have the right to be treated with respect to their personhood and not to be subjected to cruel and inhumane punishments.

Suggestions and Exercises

- Make a list of the things you did before you knew how to do them.
- Think about something about which you feel pseudocompetent. What is the developmental stage at which you should/could have learnt that easily?
- Are you primarily an intuitive, sensation, thinking or feeling type?ʾ
- Separating being and doing:
  Are you being valued for being who you are, unconditionally?
  Are you valuing other people for being who they are, unconditionally?
  Can you believe that you are a valuable member of society? What if you had an IQ of about 60, weighed 300lb and sat in front of the TV watching soap operas and game shows while masturbating and eating hamburgers for most of your life? Can such people be valued for existing, who are not doing? Note the dangerous criteria of what is valuable. Did you have difficulty with this exercise? Was it the being

or the doing aspect that gave you most trouble? Do you value the human doing or the human being?

• Differentiate the appreciation or recognition you got for doing and for being; from whom you got them, and for what.

CHAPTER FOUR

Achilles Learning

THE PSEUDOCOMPETENT STUDENT OR TRAINEE

The old man Peleus exhorted his boy Achilles always to strive for the foremost place and outdo his peers. (p. 218)

In this chapter I introduce the learning cycle and show how pseudocompetency affects people when they are learning, developing, acquiring new skills or relearning them. It is always necessary to pretend to do something before you can actually do it. We see from the learning cycle that experimenting with pseudocompetency is part of the process of learning. It only becomes a pseudocompetency problem when it becomes chronic and limits our options of developing our potential or destroys the pleasure which we could have in enjoying and developing competence. Pseudocompetency develops and remains when the natural cycle is disturbed or phases are skipped over.

Starting Out

When a baby is born it is completely unconscious of its potential capacities. It is usually considered to be an incompetent being who has some instincts and temperamental preferences, but is not capable of doing any skilful task. Very young infants are not consciously aware of all the tasks that they cannot yet fulfil, for example, using a spoon, toileting themselves, or tying their own shoes. We can imagine that as infants become aware of how an older sibling or mother ties her shoelaces or an aunt reads a story from a book they gradually become aware of all the things they cannot yet do. From a humanistic existentialist point of view, this desire to know is thought to be one of the most important driving forces in human beings – this desire to become more competent and to develop one's own sense of adequacy and autonomy in the world. As we have seen in the previous chapter, there is now accumulating research evidence to support this intuition.

The caretaking figures in a child's life – usually mother and/or father – need to be sensitive to a child's own feelings of incompetence or inadequacy as he or she begins to learn new skills and become competent at life's many tasks. The parent needs the time and patience to explain to the child step by step, so that he or she can learn in a healthy and rewarding way. If this does not happen, the child can suffer from long-lasting frustration and can acquire negative learning habits. Furthermore the child's sense of inadequacy can become reinforced, and his or her developing sense of competency and mastery permanently damaged.

'I once had a great teacher but I was in my worst Achilles phase then, and only now do I realize how good she was. I used to think, "She's being amazingly patient with me – how can I keep her placated?" I just spent all my energy in doing that and it blocked my own learning.' Children or students may become infected with a reluctance to know, an inhibition of their natural creativity, curiosity and imagination. Like many children Timothy never learnt to use his hands skilfully because, when he started building a model or exploring the inside of a clock, his father would always grab it from him, finishing the job quickly and impatiently.

This book concerns the problem which arises when this natural learning sequence is interrupted, hampered or distorted: 'I learnt how to drive a car, and got my licence, but never went on the motorway. I was never taught how to start a car, because my instructor always arrived with a warm engine.' Another person told me: 'I fell off a horse and broke my ankle. I was nervous about getting back on – I just couldn't do it. So I went back for riding lessons and discovered that I'd never learnt to ride properly.'

As a result of both personal fears, parental or educational mistakes and social threats (however subtle), many people are prevented from or inhibited in following this natural learning cycle until they feel competent and confident in their own level of knowledge, skill, or expertise.

When people do not go through the different learning stages but in some important way are allowed to, or succeed in, skipping one or more of the phases, the seeds of pseudo-competency are sown. They end up feeling they have 'faked it'. As I have discussed in Chapter 3, they may then, for example, be rewarded by promotion but psychologically penalized by internal self-doubt.

Any individualized training plan must be designed to fit the temperament, learning needs and thinking style of the pupil. It must also correct or heal any particular educational deficit or trauma they may previously have suffered. Experiences of paralysing anxiety or 'stage-fright' before leading a training or supervision session, prolonged lack of confidence, exhaustion or strain after apparently successful training or supervision, and persistent belief that 'That success was just a fluke' and 'I still think I'm a fraud and that my work colleagues or examining boards will find out that I don't really know what I'm doing' all signal the pseudocompetency syndrome referred to earlier.

Many beginning trainers or supervisors have been harmed by previous academic trauma, and they may need counselling to help heal the damage done by previous teaching or supervision. Training people with this kind of history requires great patience and sensitivity. Their natural curiosity and creativity need to be re-awakened and nurtured in their subsequent training, for these resources as well as the learning cycle are easily damaged or inhibited by neglect or abuse. Putting trainee trainers and supervisors back in touch with their own natural learning cycles always builds their confidence, self-esteem and courage to carry themselves forward.

The Learning Cycle

Many people do not know, or have forgotten, that learning is a never-ending process in a healthy organism and that learning any new skill, knowledge or behaviour goes through predictable stages. Four stages in a natural learning process have been identified[1] – how a person goes from *not knowing what they don't know* (unconscious incompetence) *to becoming aware what it is they don't know or cannot do well* (conscious incompetence), *to knowing what they know and how to do it competently* (conscious competence). This is followed by a stage where one becomes so used to *exercising one's skill or knowledge habitually* that one is hardly aware of what one is doing any more (unconscious competence). I have adapted and expanded on these four stages below.

An easier way of remembering these categories might be:

1.	The fool:	'Ignorance is bliss'
2.	The apprentice:	'I am here to learn'
3.	The master:	'I know what I know'
4.	The mechanic:	'I've forgotten how I learned'

The master is deliberately chosen as the third symbol rather than the fourth. We are used to thinking of the master as 'superior' to the mechanic – but the master who has reached the very top may start to perform automatically, moving from unconscious competence along the spiral to the stage of just performing mechanically, not knowing why he does what he does any more, unable to teach others, losing touch with the reasons or source of his actions, not picking up his own mistakes or omissions, and thus dropping into unconscious incompetence.

A good example of this learning cycle is that of driving a car. When one first tries to keep a car on the road with the steering wheel it may seem relatively easy. We have all seen youngsters pretending to drive as if it is the easiest thing in the world (this is the stage of unconscious incompetence). Because one does not yet understand all the intricacies of accelerator and clutch control, gear shifts, and brake pedal manoeuvrings, driving may seem much easier than it is at first. However, as driving lessons proceed, one can become very profoundly aware of the difficulty of co-ordinating all these different parts and activities (conscious incompetence) until one can integrate all the separate bits of the task into smoothly driving the vehicle from A to B. At the time of their driving test most people are still very aware of the particular steps that they are following, for example, looking in the mirror, depressing the clutch to change gear, and so on (conscious competence). Several years later driving has become an unconscious competency – we hardly know how we co-ordinate all the different parts and may even find it quite difficult to teach another person because we have become so used to it. It has become embedded in habit patterns of our feet, hands and mind so that we are no longer aware of them. This is the natural and healthy learning cycle when we acquire new knowledge or new skills. Of course, by the time it is so well-practised, it may become mechanical again, and possibly even dangerous because of increasing lack of care in terms of (for example) looking in the mirror. The following example comes from Muriel James.

> I concluded I am *consciously incompetent* in some ways, such as being a copy editor, as I spell poorly and sometimes refer to the 'Chicago Manual of Style' as I have never taken any writing courses myself. I am *consciously competent* in a few other ways as 17 of my own books have been published. Also, once a year I give a three-day writing workshop for people who want to have their non-fiction books published and a very high percentage of participants have been successful after taking this course.
>
> As for the other two extremes, how would I know? If they are in the unconscious then my knowledge of them is not readily available to me. However, besides being interesting, it is great fun to think about.

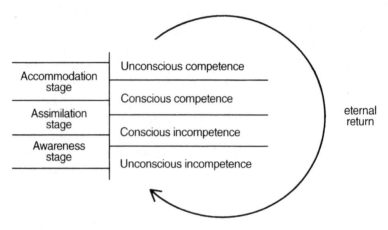

Figure 4.1 The Learning Cycle

Ways to Create a New or Different Learning Culture

People learn best when there is an atmosphere of trust that their curiosity will be welcome, their desire for mastery or competency be nurtured or educated ('brought forth' is the root meaning of 'educated'), and if they are clear that their value as human beings is not being confused with their performance. One could say that there is no deficit in being, only learning deficits. When this is part of the training or supervisory culture, people are free to engage in open dialogue or honest communication with their mentors.

It is important for trainers or supervisors to have overcome this syndrome in themselves so that they can model an openness to acknowledging their errors, ignorance and deficiencies, enthusiasm and energy for experimentation and learning through regular feedback from themselves, their peers, and their students. Trust is essential in the natural drive of human beings to learn, evolve and go through periods of constructing as well as deconstructing. Remember that many people do not enjoy positive feedback and may need reparative learning experiences in handling it. Make sure that you know the meaning that people attach to praise, and check on how they use it in small ways before making it a regular part of your repertoire with all trainees or colleagues at all times. It can be easy for a trainer or supervisor to fall into the trap of giving bright and eager students some well-intentioned praise which the students may experience as manipulative, coercive or even tyrannical, based on their past experience of teachers who abandoned the person while over-valuing the performance. Remember that people learn at different speeds and that it is important to take the time to find out what is going on, to stop and to focus on being, before re-engaging with the learning cycle.

Work with colleagues and students to make explicit what the standards for competency are at different levels for different people and at different times. People can then know as precisely as possible what they need to learn, which mistakes need to be corrected, or how to achieve a baseline of competency – if not mastery. It helps people when the task is made explicit and, where there is an overlap between being and doing, that it is regularly investigated and discussed for its safety as well as its functionality.

If you notice that people use exaggerated negative or positive self-evaluation, avoid opportunities in which they could be evaluated, or procrastinate in handing in papers or entering exams, these are all signals that your trainee may be crying out for help at the same time as experiencing difficulty in getting that help from you or the training instructor. If a trainee has difficulty in identifying when something is 'good enough' in their own work, as well as in the work of others, this is another indicator.

Phases of the Natural Learning Cycle

We can also think about the learning cycle as having three phases in addition to the four stage-posts discussed above: awareness, accommodation and assimilation. These are, of course, not exactly separate, but overlap. They are meant more as general regions which mark the learner's progress from the beginning to the more advanced stages of their own training and development. In this way they could provide some check-list for what may be needed on each part of the journey. Furthermore I do not think that learning ever ends; I see it as a life-long, cyclic process.

Awareness: from Unconscious Incompetence to Conscious Incompetence

The stage of unconscious incompetence is where the person may not even be aware of what it is that they do not know. This is why it sometimes seems that beginners have a lot of luck and also a lot of over-confidence. Awareness is bringing into consciousness the person's sense and identification of what needs to be learnt. This phase concerns the assessment of learning needs and an awareness of gaps, confusion or errors in skills and knowledge. The terminology is meant to highlight the movement from unconsciousness to consciousness in the areas which the person has to master.

If you try and avoid the incompetency part of the cycle of learning you cannot become truly competent. Incompetence can be found out. A friend said to me: 'I can't get past the initial stage when I try to paint; I can't persevere, I'm too impatient to go through this necessary stage of early and messy mistakes even though I know that if I did I could eventually create good paintings.'

Accommodation: from Conscious Incompetence to Conscious Competence

It is always necessary to pretend to do something before you can actually do it. A baby makes as if it can walk long before it actually can, and this experimenting is part of the process of learning. In this sense we are all pseudocompetent as a natural and necessary stage of learning something new. It only becomes a pseudocompetency *problem* when the pretence becomes chronic and limits people in their options of developing their potential, or destroys the pleasure which they could have in enjoying and developing their competence.

The next phase is conscious incompetence, where one is painfully aware of all the mistakes one is making and how much there is still to learn. In accommodation, the person adapts to new material which may at this stage still be experienced as foreign or different from the self, just like food which is inadequately digested. The person may take on new ideas and try them out in a mannered or stylized way without necessarily taking into account their relevance to a particular situation. This process may at times appear jerky and arrhythmic as the person explores how to accommodate themselves to the raw material, new methods or improved structures. This is a necessary stage of learning and unavoidable if one is to become truly skilful and competent in a particular area. Put simply: if you don't practise something now, you won't be able to do it in the future.

Assimilation: from Conscious Competence to Unconscious Competence

In assimilation the new learning or new skill is absorbed by the person into the self so that it is incorporated and becomes part of the self. The new skill or knowledge is integrated so that it feels natural and spontaneous, like an old habit whose origins one has forgotten. This is our 'mental metabolism'.[2] Whereas before there was some 'self-consciousness' about using newly acquired or rediscovered skills and knowledge, these are now an integral part of the person. At this stage the challenge is to maintain flexibility and variety or the 'master' may become 'mechanical', automatic or mannered. 'When I was learning to drive a car I really found out that you learn by doing. Having just passed my test, the instructor said to me, "Now you will really learn to drive".'

From Unconscious Competence to Unconscious Incompetence

The spiral of learning starts again when unconscious competence becomes unconscious incompetence.

> Because most workers become unconsciously competent in their positions, they run the danger of regressing to a state of unconscious incompetency – a sort of occupational senility brought on by overt complacency on the part of the worker. This state, of course, is more symptomatic of the type of worker who has no desire to keep updated on his craft or field, who sees no need for additional study once he has learned his trade. Because of this attitude, he is vulnerable to 'unconscious incompetency' and can easily regress to the point where he is, for all practical purposes, an unconscious incompetent.
>
> This eventual gravitation on the part of the unconsciously competent employee toward unconscious incompetency underlines the need for continuous training and retraining programs. As in professional sports, this often means that the player must be retrained in the fundamentals of his game in order to make him consciously competent again.
>
> *And only the consciously competent can train the conscious incompetent, or bring the unconscious incompetent to an awareness of his backsliding.*[3]

Pseudocompetency is a major threat causing or precipitating mid-life crisis. In middle age, the discrepancy between worldly acknowledgement and inner experience can hit you hard. Mid-life is a peak time for testing and challenging the façade you've built up over your true self. People either cover up even more during this period, the cost of which is enormous, or react strongly to throw over everything they had done and been before. Then they often say: 'I feel much more real.' But it may not be the most mature move because it goes from one pole right to the other; missing out the middle phase and choosing to return to the beginning of development, learning again from scratch something different, because it's less scary. Good drivers may not be able to pass their driving test again. Being unconsciously incompetent means incorporating mistakes without being aware of them; so we have to become aware of the areas of incompetence that have become embedded in our competence.

The Learning Cycle Recommences

From what has been said here, it must be clear that the learning cycle never ends. To expand and develop as a person one must always start new things; it is too comfortable and stagnant sticking with what is known. There can hardly be a final product or an accomplished steady state in any discipline which continues to evolve and which demands of its practitioners continued flexibility and willingness to keep developing. As soon as one cycle is completed, another one begins. In my view this is natural. It is not a compulsive, externally motivated search for mystical perfection, it is more a natural organismic urge to grow and develop and to become more skilled, more understanding and more compassionate. Being in touch with this evolutionary drive in ourselves enables competent and excellent people to continue growing and changing. Lots of people have spots of pseudocompetency in their lives, and we all have stages of pseudocompetency as we start out at the beginning of a new learning process.

Figure 4.1 shows how the cyclic nature of learning and its various phases mirror the cyclic nature of all experience. All experience goes in phases: from microscopic cycles such as the biological functions of warming up or cooling down, to the macroscopic cycles such as the sequences of adult developmental stages, which may take a lifetime. Larger and smaller cycles can be managed creatively and satisfactorily if the natural processes are allowed to reach their organismic conclusion.

Many people have found the learning cycle very helpful, especially the part about learning and unlearning, then moving on to knowing things in a different and deeper way. We can all take comfort from knowing we have this internal recycling process; even the person who learnt it and then somewhat despairingly said, 'You mean I'm always going to keep learning like this? Just when I thought it was safe to go back to work!'

Advanced trainers learn to recognize their own authority and ability, and so model excellence and appreciation of their own worth to their trainees. They also take on the responsibility to train and educate less experienced trainers through a system of apprenticing beginners. Younger people can see experienced trainers as they train. In this way the experienced trainers can get valuable feedback on what they do well, so that they can later articulate this to others. This will also prevent experienced trainers from remaining in the area of *unconscious competence* where they become mechanical and are no longer able to identify or pass on their skills. An apprentice often gives far more reliable feedback than can be got from group members, because the apprentice is view-ing the process both from the perspective of a trainer and from that of a trainee. It is as if they 'see the stitching on the back of the piece of lovely embroidery' and can thus fully appreciate the care and delicacy invested in the finished product.

Pseudocompetency, Lying and Apology

Pseudocompetency is not about deliberately lying – and yet the internal guilt and the shame arise from the feeling that one is somehow being untruthful. It is different from pathological lying, which is about making up stories on every occasion. The one is intentionally deceptive, the other is caught in a web of unrealistic expectations and natural aspirations, compounded by fact that the teachers are covering up. In a way, if only the pseudocompetent could find a little more self-deception and believe others' opinions of them, they would be a lot happier!

Pathological apology is pre-emption of somebody finding you out – like an Achilles actually extending his heel and saying, 'This is the spot.' A mother may apologize for a fine family meal, saying it is not as well-cooked as she had hoped, and she had run out of some ingredient. It is different from lying. In lying the intention is to deceive the others. Pseudo-competency is more like a trap. You are trying to get out of it but other people are also holding you in it, and to get out you will have to activate the learning cycle once again, getting more and more desperate that nobody will believe you.

Suggestions and Exercises

- Cycles: everything natural moves in cycles. List the important things you have to keep doing over and over again (a) to make life viable and (b) to make life worthwhile. This stops you getting stale.
- Teach someone something. Notice how you do it. Get their feedback.
- Get someone to teach you something. Everyone has something to teach. How does the dialogue between you and the teacher work?
- List some ways in which you could make yourself feel smart or brave before you do difficult things for yourself.
- 'Don't teach people who feel stupid – make them feel smart first and then teach them.' In other words, do not make them feel inferior by letting them know how much you know. List some ways of finding those comfortable spaces where you feel smart or clever when teaching, so that the desire for learning flowers in other people.
- Identify the most important skills you have learned in your life, and then identify the optimum conditions under which you learn. For example, do you like frequent appreciation, frequent criticism? Do you like your teacher to be very involved or very far away? Do you want many small rewards frequently, or a substantial reward at the end of it? Do you learn best experientially (through doing), through reading, through hearing, or through watching? Do you need frequent breaks or do you like having an intense concentration? Do you like rehearsals and exercises or do you feel you carry the understanding in your head?

• Identify the messages you may have been given as a child that now drive you in some way. Whose voices are they? Are they true to your own? If not, what would be the 'allowing' messages you would prefer to live by? The following table[4] maybe useful.

Drivers	Permissions
Be perfect	It's OK to be yourself
Hurry up	It's OK to take your time
Try hard	It's OK to do it
Please me	It's OK to consider yourself and respect yourself
Be strong	It's OK to be open and to take care of yourself

• i) Identify an educational trauma, such as any time, occasion or person which interfered with, damaged or neglected your natural learning process.
ii) Identify resentment you may still hold about this, any shame or guilt and an excuse you have derived from it.
• Make a list of the basic things you need to know about the area you need to grow competent in, for example: how not to know (how to behave when you don't know), how to be held, how not to apologize for not knowing, how to feed yourself. How do you know when something is wrong?
• Think of a competency – something you can repeat frequently, without undue strain, and which you *and* other people think that you do competently or excellently. Now think of the process by which you learnt that competency. Be as specific as possible about the conditions surrounding your learning. Who was there? Was the teacher present or absent? What was the modelling? What was the balance between negative and positive feedback? Was it primarily visual, auditory or kinaesthetic learning? Did you achieve it overnight, in gradual stages, in leaps and bounds, in solid concentration over a long period, with other people or alone, in co-operation or competition? Did the envy

or obsequiousness of other people motivate or incapacitate you? What were the learning features of the situation? What is important about the 'hows' of the ways in which you learnt to achieve competency and mastery? Keep the notes that you make on this and review them whenever you need to learn something new. Know what your own optimum learning conditions are.

- How do you relate to teachers? Do you let them in, diminish them, over-value them, introject them? Do you use them to persecute yourself or support yourself? Do you trust them?
- Describe an incident in which you taught something to someone and then deduce from this the way you would like to be taught. We all teach the way we would like to learn. It is very important to teach our teachers how to teach us.
- Is it inevitable in the learning process that, once you have become consciously competent, you will become unconsciously incompetent? How will you go about becoming your own supervisor?
- Are you on the way to achieving the three objectives which you set yourself at the end of the preface? What would be the next step you need to take to move nearer to completing them?

CHAPTER FIVE

Achilles at Work

THE PSEUDOCOMPETENT EXECUTIVE

Achilles the great runner gave him a black look. 'You shameless schemer,' he cried, 'always aiming at a profitable deal! How can you expect any of the men to give you loyal service when you send them on a raid or into battle? . . . The truth is that we joined the expedition to please you . . . a fact which you utterly ignore.' (p. 27)

This chapter specifically focuses on current organization culture and how it encourages and maintains large-scale pseudocompetency among the workforce, particularly among the senior people in the organization. This is based on extensive experience of working as an organizational consultant and trainer to large organizations and to their own trainers and consultants.

Achilles the Executive

As a counsellor and psychotherapist, I have become increasingly aware of the large-scale disruptive impact that current world conditions have upon my clients, most of whom are well-functioning and intelligent professionals. As an organizational consultant, I am increasingly perturbed by the depression, fear, anger and bitter disillusionment of many people with the organizations for which they work, or from which they are being 'out-placed' or being made 'redundant'.

The following conversation between client and therapist is typical of Achilles at work:

> A: I'm scared at work. Scared of talking and having people take me seriously. I've got to perform, doing something I'm not sure I can do.
> B: If people take you seriously you have to perform relentlessly at that level.
> A: I can't keep it up because I'm not allowed to not know something.
> B: But at some point or another you are going to come across something you don't know!

Managers and developers need to enable themselves and empower others to survive these turbulent, unpredictable conditions and transform them into opportunities for survival, if not growth. The natural human need for security, control, certainty, and predictability is denied again and again as institutions go out of business and economic conditions fluctuate unpredictably. What used to be a reasonable expectation, for example, a lifetime of employment, is now constantly under review. Even the last bastions of the public sector can no longer be sure of this.

I repeatedly hear people say:

> We just don't know what sort of job we will have in the future, or in a few months' time. There seems to be no leadership. We are given impossible tasks. Our targets are increased, resources lowered, employer expectations seem to be escalating, and we feel crazy because we're expected to do what cannot be achieved.

I am reminded of Pavlov's dogs who were rewarded for successfully differentiating between an ellipse and a circle; as the experimenters gradually shaped the ellipses into circles and the circles into ellipses, the dogs experienced the impossibility of the task and essentially went mad. This is how some people describe their working conditions now.

At the same time as such conditions of precariousness, uncertainty and stressful anxiety become the norm for a very large section of our working population (including the top managers) there is an escalation in complexity on all fronts which may leave us feeling even more de-skilled. As one person said, 'Even if you don't change, change is being foisted on you.' Continuity is over, and the 'management of change' has become a contradiction in terms. Long-range unpredictability has become the norm and the only constant now is change itself. An Achilles workshop for managers left one participant feeling sick and unconnected as she examined the personal cost of her professional pseudocompetency: 'I was making the hurdles higher and higher. Last year I did not jump it – I crashed spectacularly. Looking back, my greatest sense was relief; it would have given me a promotion I was not ready for.'

The Need to Make Meaning

The two most basic psychological needs of human beings are to work and to love. Work is one of the most important ways of gaining our sense of efficacy or competency in the world. Human beings need to feel competent and useful in their working lives to maintain and develop a sense of self, of mastery and of competency. As we saw earlier in the book, child development researchers are now confirming what common sense has always known – people need to make some kind of useful contribution to the world in order to maintain their self-esteem. The need to make this kind of meaning out of our time on earth is apparently universal and unrelenting, although the definition of work is of course very wide – it may be housekeeping, caring for an elderly parent, voluntary service or the creation of a multi-million dollar business empire, doing a newspaper round or finishing a crossword, making poetry or singing in a choir. When we lose this sense of making a valuable contribution, people often get depressed, and may even lose the will to live. Some old people's homes where sad grandfathers and grandmothers sit listlessly staring at a TV screen show what a depletion in vitality and self-esteem can be caused when people no longer feel they are valued for their part in the community.

When people are deprived of the opportunity to work through their feelings, retirement, redundancy or loss of a job, the psychological damages are profound. Statistics have shown how many men die within two years of retirement – a shocking figure. It may relate to the fact that many of these men report that, although they may be happy to stop the pressures and strains of their work, they miss the company at work, the social side, the feeling of being significant to others, the challenges which they used to resent, but which gave them a sense of achievement and satisfaction. Suddenly to be at home all the time with no one really needing your opinion or energy except the grandchildren on some weekends leads painfully to meaninglessness and despair for those who can't make another life after 60.

The equivalent of this in women's experience has in the past been called the 'Empty Nest Syndrome'. This phrase is used to describe the female sense of void and futility once the children have left home. However much the mother may have grumbled about clearing up messes or chauffeuring to college, the sense of silence and sterility can be overwhelming once the children are gone and she suddenly feels that nobody needs her any longer except an ageing husband. Women at this stage often look to the emotional support of a partner only to find that over the past years of child-rearing they have simply grown apart, and now without a family to discuss there is nothing left to say.

It matters most to human beings to feel that their lives make some kind of difference to others, that there is meaning to their existence, that they can answer the question 'What am I doing here?' in some kind of personally significant way. The psychological, economic and social ravages of redundancy in some parts of Western Europe have created a veritable industry in counselling services related to employment, re-employment and self-marketing. These all focus on – and sometimes exploit – the human horror of empty hours and a meaningless existence. As we have seen, being accepted for just being yourself as a person is essential, and should not be confused with being valued for your production or contribution.

I remember one horror story of a man who kept pretending to go to work each day for several years, while making up stories to tell his chronically ill wife and borrowing money from friend after friend to look after his son in a psychiatric hospital. He kept the fact of his job dismissal successfully from his family in this way, but at enormous psychological cost to himself and to the integrity of his relationships. He collapsed of a heart attack in a café one day. It was only when the hospital phoned his home that his wife discovered the well-meaning deception he had carried out every day for so many years to safeguard her from the bad news.

The costs of loss of work are enormous. As we have seen, losing a job can mean you lose status, money, company (both social and collegial), strokes, meaning and value in our society all at one go. A man who loses his job is in a time of great need for support and companionship, yet one such man told me that he could not face going to the pub to see his friends because they all knew he had lost his job. He could not even face their sympathy, he felt so bad. Yet these were in fact the people he could probably count on for support, advice and networking towards finding the next job.

Creating a Good Impression

As one top management trainer said to me:

> As I realize that I am acquiring a 'good' reputation professionally, I feel an equal mixture of pleasure and fear. In paying attention to the whole of my person, including the feelings in my body, I began to realize the difference between pseudocompetency and created competency.

Many people have difficulty admitting this. Most people don't know that there is any alternative to pseudocompetency because many of our educational and training programmes train people in pseudocompetency. Many parents, trainers and teachers themselves are pseudocompe-tent, so it is a self-fulfilling cycle. A police officer told me how, in his view, pseudocompetency in his organization had be-come institutionalized, for people were not staying in one job long enough to learn how to become fully competent at it before moving on within the organization.

In the current professional climate there is enormous in-terest in professionalization. Many structures are being created for judging competence as objectively as possible in various fields by boards, groups, and examination struc-tures. Increasing professionalization is evident in most fields of human endeavour. Accompanying this is a growing ap-preciation of and even legal insistence on reaccreditation in the professions, and annual competency reviews in organi-zations. So it is no longer the case that people can train or qualify and be considered competent for all their lives. There is even discussion about regular *retesting* to establish compe-tency to drive a car. These initiatives may be partly in response to the recognition that conscious competency is a stage in an ongoing learning cycle which almost inevitably fades into unconscious incompetence unless skills are reviewed, attitudes re-assessed and knowledge updated.

Of course, along with this enhanced interest in profession-alization, externally assessed competency criteria and re-accreditation, there is now a growing disquiet among many professionals which they find hard, if not impossible, to admit. This may partly be a defence against the fear of pseudocompetence. It also simply places the fear elsewhere, such as, 'Will I be in or out of the socially agreed-to-be-competent group?' To be a top manager in many commercial competitive organizations means that you know how to manage in all ways at all times. You would never show that you feel inadequate, insecure and full of doubt about your capacity to do parts of your job.

Organizational trainers, managers and workers have told me that on training courses it is frequently considered shameful to admit that you don't know how to manage, how to motivate people, or how to resolve interpersonal conflicts.

Of course it is very hard to train people to be better at something if they are not even prepared to admit that there is room for improvement! Business cultures easily collude, making it difficult, if not impossible, for people to go through the different and difficult phases of learning:

> When people see what I can do, I think inside 'Oh no, not you as well!' I've learned now to say no to people. Before, I was sending out very powerful invitations to people to say 'You can do it'. Now I have learned to function well under stress, even if I'm ill-prepared. That too is a cover-up.

'Competence' in such organizations comes to mean the way in which you hide the fear of being in a situation in which your competency is being judged. Some people mistake competency itself for whether or not you can give an 'acceptably polished' performance. If you can 'fake it', then that makes you a good professional. Whether or not we actually know the job is sometimes considered less important than *creating the impression* that we know the job. A key concern at interviews of a company's hiring team is: Is this person acceptably professional in the commercial environment? Much discussion (in management consultancy as well as in other forms of sales) is devoted to the presenting persona of the management consultant or the salesperson:

> I put together some community programmes. They were basically OK but they had no depth. I never wrote it up because I couldn't – I didn't have the backing or the understanding of what I was doing. It looked good but if you'd put your hand through there would have been nothing behind it, and it's such a shame because what I did was good but. . . . Internally I knew that I was cheating. I knew that I was getting away with things all the time, but I felt good because I felt like I was one of them and getting a lot of satisfaction and strokes.

What is often being judged is how you deal with the reality of covering up your inadequacies and insecurities; basically, how well you can create an impression, or an acceptable façade. A consultant told me: 'Many organizations have bought into the Emperor's new clothes syndrome; and yet every person knows the others are bullshitting.' This is pseudocompetency and how it is maintained in organizational life. I have also encountered several high-powered executives who are very embarrassed by the fact that they do not have degrees. They then attempt to hide, lie, or buy degrees to compensate for this imagined inadequacy.

The taboo is on discussing what you don't know, admitting the flaw. Doing so proves you are incompetent, so nobody speaks out. Wanting to talk about it in order to get help, you feel trapped in the pretence and eaten up by the anxiety of being found out. 'On no account say that anything is an experiment – we are not trying out anything – we know what we are doing, and this must be adhered to.' 'We simply can't accept trial and error.' Delegates to top European business training schools have said: 'We have to keep what we don't know hidden even from ourselves.' Another executive said:

> I used to say to myself, I know some things and not everything – then the working day becomes stimulating. When I act in that way, I think that I'm working in an environment where people are acting in the opposite way. It's threatening to me. When I don't know what I'm doing here I look indecisive, and it's not OK to be like that. It's difficult and damaging. I was made redundant recently.

Pseudocompetency often has more hold in the executive and professional groups where there is a lot of space for cover-up. There may even be a closing of the ranks to protect pseudo-competent colleagues of the same professional body because everybody fears their own inadequacies may be exposed if a fine toothcomb is to be taken to anyone in the community. Most people feel that they have covered up or skipped over some area in developing and getting recognition for their expertise. Both the medical profession and politicians are frequently accused of just such professional collusion to protect incompetent colleagues; and sometimes it may be true.

> I remember the anger when I was five at seeing my school report say how mature and independent I was. This is also the

damaging aspect of organizational culture. I was appointed to train trainers. I felt in need of some training myself, so I approached my manager but he immediately said 'No, you don't need that, from what I've seen. You do it very well.' His good opinion of me was destroying me.

In business there is a need to go back and learn the *same* things, or the *basic* things again. How rarely this is presented and understood. What shame there would be in going back to re-take the early exams again! And how can we turn around and ask for what we are already supposed to possess, and to be using every day? It is hard enough for some workers even to ask for what would be sensible to learn, as some older workers have found in struggling to understand the new computer technology that their younger colleagues grew up with. As one executive put it:

> When I have applied for jobs and then got them on the basis that I am competent, I simply don't have the option of asking to go back to basics, to get some training. I've dug myself a hole. But what else could I have done to get that job?

A colleague told how she applied for a job in Australia. This vacancy was for a level 4 social worker, which is the highest, but she didn't understand the numbered levels because Britain didn't have them. She thought it was the lowest so she applied. They just couldn't believe the cheek – that she had actually sent her CV without ever looking into the system. They called her to interview because they wanted to see the person that could do a thing like that. They asked what she had thought when she saw this advert and what were the skills she'd offer if they gave it to her. Anyway she got the job – they gave her a job as a welfare worker until she got her degree, then she could become a social worker. They helped her through her course and had her assisting a social worker which was very good for her – this is a real example where she could talk her way through that interview and pull the wool over their eyes, and she did – in some way she really did.

As a trainer I have often noticed that there are few applicants to introductory courses, and many applicants to the courses billed as 'advanced' even though the same ground may be covered. The tendency is to assume that we have grasped the basics – and we may not even be giving ourselves a chance to know what the basics are.

Long-range Planning May Not Help

The situation is considerably worse even than the perpetuation in the present of organizational cultures which encourage self-deception, bluffing your way to get the credits and a whole ethos which suggests that we can know everything.[1] A multinational corporation with a turnover of £30 billion had an unpredictable and inexplicable drop in sales of 25% in one week, from which it never recovered. People in business and organizations report an escalation of similar or worse situations, making it more and more impossible to do the kind of long-range planning that was considered highly desirable some years ago.

Management theoreticians like Stacey consider 5- and 10-year plans as nonsense, that the process of preparing plans for the long-term can even be harmful. Current awareness that everything is changing very rapidly and unpredictably creates huge anxiety. Putting out a plan is a defence against this anxiety, but it is also very harmful as it can restrict the learning process. Many management and strategic consultants have discovered that creating long-term plans does act more as a defence against self-doubt and uncertainty in this way. When reminded of their stated plans and actually retrieving the documents created at the time it was frequently found that people had done completely different things – often to their own surprise.

People have found it much more useful to create and discuss different future scenarios. Such as I believe BP did, in considering the fact that crude oil might suddenly increase in price dramatically and unpredictably. When the situation in the Gulf occurred they were prepared. Most managers do not take 5-year forecasts seriously any more. This is a move away from rigidity towards flexibility and a recurrent admission that we should always be learning (and unlearning). However, as many of us working as managers and organizational consultants have found, it is very risky to stand up and say 'I do not know what is going on and I am not preparing plans.' Of course your clients will want to get rid of you. You have to go through incredible smoothing-over actions to pretend to know what is going on. We have to participate in this kind of pretence because the majority of people are looking through an old-fashioned Newtonian lens. Some of us are starting to see through the new lens; but we have to keep it quiet because others will get too frightened if conventional wisdom were fundamentally questioned. Moult had the rare courage to write in a management journal, 'We don't know what is happening and we don't know what we are doing.'[2] This could be the beginning of developing true competence in learning.

Gossip in Organizations

This atmosphere of confusion can easily lead people to pretend they know things, which is one of the grounds for gossip. This can be particularly damaging within organizations. If we are frightened of not knowing what is going on, we take little snippets of information and construct a reality on the basis of these morsels. Gossips are frightened to approach anyone and ask 'What exactly is going on?' because the version they have heard may be based on one person's hypothesis or fear and have no relation to the facts at all. They may want to look powerful as holders of confidential knowledge, and being 'in the know' may also make them sought after and praised by colleagues. Or they may have had a bad experience of approaching someone once in this way, offering the version of the story that they have, and being severely criticized or laughed at for believing such outlandish notions.

Changing the Organizational Rules

A courageous organizational consultant told me:

> I was asked to train people as out-placement counsellors. I'd be paid quite a lot for a 3-day contract to train them to deal with people who had lost their jobs. I discovered that all the people who were assigned to this course had been made redundant themselves. I thought it was unethical and I told the management, explained to them . . . it was the culture that needed confronting.

I was told about a manager in the retail industry who is experienced as chaotic and erratic – but people who have trained with him have a reputation for being much more resourceful and in demand than the rest in their other companies. There are many jokes about him 'still having a job', but the people who can stand the pace talk of an atmosphere of excitement, uncertainty and creativity – anything but a 'holding environment' – which is always or mostly false. Until now, management has been all about control; now it is about change and paradox. Given the current state of our world, it is probably far more helpful in the long run to facilitate people and teach them how to work with chaos, disorder and the unpredictable than to strive for false security. The old style of management does not equip people for the real world, but instead builds a dependency on these grandiose promises of stability in a world which is essentially unstable and creative rather than rule-bound.

On encountering the notion of pseudocompetency, people are often tempted to apply it as a way of understanding other people, or as a diagnostic tool. This would not be correct since the idea concerns a subjective experience; it is really the experience of a mismatch between how confident a person feels and how they appear to perform any assessment. It is for the person concerned in the privacy of their own heart. We should consider the major part played by the workplace in fostering pseudocompetency in the working context. Our society has inherited organizations characterized by shame and shaming systems from a male-dominated culture. Indeed, shaming is probably the greatest single cause of pseudocompetency in the workplace. Shaming is often a covert strategy adopted by the organization in the false belief that the fear of shame will make people perform more efficiently. Experience has shown that motivations based on fear may work in the short-term; but in the long-term they are more often than not highly dysfunctional. Shame is also used within some of the more competitive working environments as a way of exercising power and control. It would thus be counter to the spirit and intention of this book to apply the term pseudocompetent to colleagues at work, since this may be helping to create the very condition of shame that fosters pseudocompetency in the first place.

Suggestions and Exercises

- What are your organization's stated goals and objectives? Are they generally believed in and furthered by the staff, or do staff just toe the line to humour or placate the bosses?
- List the organizational skills you have learnt. How many are true group skills and how many are for survival in a collusively pseudocompetent atmosphere?
- How do you behave in your staff room or common room? Do you feel free to swear, for example, or feel a need to hold your tongue? Do you have an image to keep up?
- Make a list of ways in which you could gracefully refuse to join in gossip in your organization.

CHAPTER SIX

Achilles as Parent

THE PSEUDOCOMPETENT MOTHER/FATHER/ CARE-GIVER

'My son, my son!' said Thetis, bursting into tears. 'Was it for this I nursed my ill-starred child?' (p. 34)

In this chapter I explore how parents may get caught in the pseudocompetency trap. Illustrations from real life and counselling practice are given. Parents may play-act, not knowing what to do for their family. This breeds pseudocompetency as the children learn from what they see, or try to take over the (emotional) care-taking themselves.

Achilles as Parent

Pseudocompetency in parents is probably one of the world's most closely guarded secrets. Parents are 'supposed to know' and children can feel terribly let down and disappointed when they see their parents fail, be shown up or be humiliated by others. It is usually disillusioning to see the humanity of those we admire. It is maturity to feel gratitude for the virtues and compassion for the flaws.

I have many counselling clients who remember painfully how their fathers were subservient to their bosses, saying 'Yes Sir' when men younger but in more powerful positions gave instructions or advice as if they were the ones who really knew the answers. Infants want and, like little animals, *need* to believe that their parents will feed them appropriately and take the best possible care of them. It is frightening and disturbing to discover anything to the contrary.

> I had to lie. If I didn't know something my mother would make my not knowing into something all right, so that she didn't feel stranded with a helpless lump. If I was naughty at school she wouldn't discipline me or tell me what was appropriate or inappropriate, but would stroke me and say: 'You're such a character.' She'd be proud of this fighting child who was a character instead of a moody wimp – it became more important, whatever I did, to find the good in it to keep herself feeling OK – she redefined whatever I did. So in terms of my pseudocompetency I thought, 'I'm OK really whatever I do, I can fudge it or pull the wool over people's eyes because I'll just be a character – if I'm not too brainy then I'll be a character or be cute.' Somehow I'd find a compensating way of being, and think that was competency.

Another person told how his mother insisted that he eat a certain babyfood. He kept spitting it out, and mother kept forcing the child. It was only when a servant intervened that the baby's body wisdom was proved right. The food had been poisoned and the baby would have died had he eaten it. The same mother later fell asleep at the wheel of the car, and again the child nearly died. His adult life has been a constant struggle against his own pseudocompetency, taking care of disturbed children professionally and gaining a reputation for giftedness in this field while regularly sweating with fear and being filled with anxiety and paralysing self-criticism before he goes into the school.

Of course these early survival fears get confused with current concerns about earning a living. He fears that someone will find out that inside he is only a little boy pretending to know how to take care of the other children. Worst of all, he realizes that he himself does not genuinely have the necessary skills, knowledge, competencies or confidence to do this kind of work. His truly competent colleague seems to do twice as many hours with half the stress – perhaps because she does not have such a high reputation to live up to, perhaps because she has learned the scope as well as the limits of her abilities. No wonder this client is so tired and stressed after his brilliant performances as a teacher of such disturbed children that he cannot give his wife the kind of attention and care one adult can deserve to expect from another. It is not that his gifts are not real. It is more that the cost of continuing to display these gifts without the proper substructures is constantly eroding both his confidence and his pleasure in his work, as well as his ability to be *real* as a person and as a lover.

Let's Play Mummies and Daddies

There is often a sense of play-acting as mothers and fathers. So many mothers pretend that they know what they are doing in bringing up children, especially if they never had a clear model. They learn through acting but then the environment starts to assign them a role as a good parent. They know they aren't and they panic.

A paediatrician well known in her field as an expert sat on the floor of her home surrounded with textbooks, and wept in despair at the screaming of her new baby. 'I am a doctor in this field and I haven't a clue how to deal with this baby,' she cried, frantically turning the pages and trying to find the most basic of information, which seemed strangely elusive.

Many pseudocompetent children have pseudocompetent parents who may be gifted in some ways and quite incompetent in others but, instead of getting some help with the incompetency, they organize their lives around hiding or compensating for it. Then the children learn how to do this as well and the parents are reluctant to admit that the child may need to learn the very basics of something. Pseudocompetency can spread throughout the family as an overt or unspoken rule over many years: 'I found out years later once we'd all grown up that all three of us children broke our little toe without anyone knowing.'

Our children reflect our inadequacies, since they confront us both with their desire to know and our inability to teach from our own experience or to admit that we don't know ourselves. If the parents cover it up, then it is very likely that they will invite their children to cover up as well.

As a child my father came into my room one day looking nervous and asked me straight out: 'Um, do you reckon you know all there is to know about sex then?' He looked strained, as if he wanted me to say 'yes'. I felt he was prompting me in some way. So of course, hoping to please him, I said 'Yes, Dad', even though I didn't have much of a clue. 'Good, that's all right then,' he said abruptly and hurried out.

It is not hard to imagine that this was some kind of replay from the sex education he got from his father. Many years later this young woman got married and told her friend: 'I won't get pregnant – I take precautions.' Three months later she was pregnant. The friend asked how this was possible if she took precautions.

What kind of prevention had she used? She said: 'We never climax together and that was the prevention.' It was hard to believe that this was the twentieth century. Parents pass pseudocompetency on to their children, both by example and by neglecting to teach them in the appropriate way about the most important things in life, such as loving, fighting, failing, crying, creating.

Many clients have sat in tears with me saying, 'I am still much of a child myself. How can I possibly be a parent to another youngster who will be looking to me for guidance?' There are at least two ways in which this can go wrong. One is by the parent behaving pseudocompetently, as we have seen in some of the above examples with the parents pretending knowledge and expertise they do not really feel. The other is if the parent burdens the child with their own ignorance and inadequacy, somehow expecting the child to give them the comfort, reassurance and education. For example, Mariel's mother frequently wept at home and took drugs, saying that she just didn't know how to balance the cost of feeding her family. Mariel learnt early that budgeting for the housekeeping would be his job, and that the first outgoing to be allowed for would be the cocaine. Then these children grow up as pseudocompetent adults because they have been taking care of their parents in this way.

The Ambitious Parent

Ali, now adult, saw a clear link with the Achilles archetype in the tension between him and his mother's ambitions: 'She wanted to have a son like a god who would take care of his mother perfectly. It gave me unrealistic expectations of myself . . . of being more than mortal.' Another adult told sadly that: 'My mother couldn't stand the idea that I might not be able to do something.' This is an exact replica of Thetis dipping Achilles in the river Styx, which was done out of genuine pride and love but which made her the true author of his flaw. And Achilles cannot learn how to protect himself, because he is an immortal yet a man who can be killed he is caught in a double bind from which he can only escape by admitting his vulnerability and then learning how to protect himself appropriately.

It is common for people with pseudocompetent adaptations to have had parents with high ambitions for them, whether to gain a top profession or to become outstanding or famous in some way. Shirley Temple's mother is an example of how to create pseudocompetent children. Some of the children who reach the top, even though genuinely gifted, can only operate using the prop of drugs and alcohol. It is important to remember that children are often flattered to be treated as adults before their time, they want the praise and flattery of 'You don't have to be taught, you're a natural.' Then later, as adults, they ask 'If I am a natural why am I so scared? There must be something wrong with me!'

As one trainee put it: 'I want to be taught the things that I was too clever to learn when they were taught the first time.' If this sort of honesty is not found deep in the Achilles heart, then the cycle recommences, and the vicious pattern often gets passed on to their own children in turn. But we have to keep our wits about us:

> My father was more adult in terms of coping in the professional world but that's where a lot of my pseudocompetence also came from. The adult programming from him was: 'You can learn and be a professional like me but actually underneath I'm crazy.' So he showed me how to be a professional. You go out and be professional but then you come home and you're crazy or you can only have very short spates of professionalism, you couldn't hold out for long. He could be at a 4-day conference for a day, then he'd have to leave, and he couldn't come back. He didn't have the ego strength to hold onto his professionalism, yet no one caught him out. If you have such a polished exterior then nobody is going to call your bluff. He would say to me 'I feel such a failure. You have such expectations of me and I find it so stressful because underneath I feel so sick.' My father talked very openly about his sickness – it was about confession. That's how he got me to also take care of him. Because I found it very difficult to be angry with him when he was so honest.

This person clearly saw the danger that some pseudocompetent parents may abdicate responsibility and expect the child to take care of them emotionally, if not physically. In this case the father was disarmingly honest to his child about his pseudocompetence as a parent, while still covering up at work. More often, parents will continue to cover up and hand this tendency on to their children in turn.

The Anxiety of Ignorance, and the Agony of Shame

There is great anxiety of *not knowing* in our culture, and the shame of admitting that you don't know; how vulnerable you are to being laughed at. Culturally, it is like a pernicious infection. Until we learn how to celebrate the desire to learn, and to ensure the necessary tools and atmosphere for learning, the damage will be perpetuated. Everyone must be seen to know what to do when everyone is pretending, and no one is safe from the pressure. In some faraway cultures such as the Baka pygmies, shaming and humiliation by laughter is the tribe's primary way of controlling behaviour – being pointed and jeered at is one of the worst punishments, especially if it is done by children. Is this so far away from the shaming in the kindergarten down the road, or at your dinner table?

Pseudocompetent Playtime

Many parents are also pseudocompetent at playing with their children. Frequently their parents had never played with them. In their anxiety to explain things they may over-intellectualize and treat the children as adults before they are ready to learn on that level. On the other hand they may consciously try to play and appear only tense, heavy-handed and inauthentic to the child, who is quick to pick up these signals. They may play only strongly competitive games, or impose strict punishments and threats. They may give prizes only for performance or winning. They may want to win so badly that the child always has to lose.

There are settings in which therapists work with parents on how to play with their children. If you have never learnt how to play, or your natural abilities to play have been damaged, you may need to go right back to basics and re-learn them from someone else. Playing is a natural form of learning, for young animals and children. We learn through play to explain the world to ourselves, to use our bodies, improve co-ordination and reflexes. Playing is a child's work and an adult's re-creation. It is the very matrix for creativity of any kind.

The 'Good Enough' Parent

Unless we have internalized a 'good enough' parent inside ourselves, it is very difficult indeed to be a good enough parent to our own children.

> With Mum, it goes right back to when I was born. She told me she was determined to have another girl because she wanted Stella to have a sister so we could have the relationship she had

never had. Stella was about five, a very difficult child and Mum had no relationship with her and didn't love her – she found it very difficult to love this child that she had created, it felt like a monster to her. So when I was born – that was the first birth that my father had been at, he hadn't been at the other two – and I was a little girl and they could now stop having children and she'd got what she wanted. So I think that's when she started this 'specialness' which she put on me.

As children, most of us remember vowing that we would never ever treat our children in the way that our parents did. For example, Jim swore than he would never call his son stupid in an angry and humiliating voice, as his father had done to him. Then one day to his chagrin, he 'found himself' shouting at his son in the very same tone of voice and the very words his father had used on him. Fortunately, he had done much work on himself in personal counselling and quickly became aware of his behaviour and stopped it.

The following vivid description comes from a care worker feeling the desire to kill a child and recognizing that this is the way her own mother felt about her:

> I hold it all in, the scary moments with children. In the past, I have been judgemental about other people who have admitted that they want to hit children. I ran a bath for one boy and suddenly had an overwhelming urge to drown him. My whole body was tense; he had been on at me for 3 days. There was just me and five kids in the house. I could *feel* the pleasure of drowning him. I phoned the resident psychiatrist who told me it was all right to feel like that, to breathe deeply and release it. The boy left 6 months later and the relief – I couldn't work with him again because of the deep guilt I felt that even the thought was abusive, and I felt he could sense it.

We all have faithful 'psycho-video' recordings inside ourselves, not only of what our parents said to us – the messages they gave, the taboos they imposed, the threats and seductions with which they manipulated us but also of their fear and worries, their own internal self-abusing and self-critical voices, their fears of loss of control and their desires to survive or to kill themselves in despair.

Children absorb their parents or their significant early caretaking figures in many ways, and they become like a kind of other personality within the child and, of course, later, the adult. These feelings, attitudes and behaviours have been described as the inner parent. This inner parent represents the real parent figures and can be voluntarily or involuntarily stimulated to act upon the here-and-now of our lives. Under stress or when we are tired, a challenge arises to all our good resolutions to be better parents to our own children than our own parents were to us. Far too often we reproduce the very patterns that we rejected.

Changing Views of Parenting

Since the beginning of this century parents have been increasingly bombarded with theories and information which have led to the idea of bad parenting being blamed for most of what is wrong in the world. It may be hard to remember that in previous times God, the devil, bad genes and other forces were used to explain adult misbehaviour, illness and evil. Nowadays many people want to avoid damaging our children and seriously want to learn how to be better parents so as to give our kids better chances than we had. This becomes another kind of pernicious pressure to perform. A newspaper recently quoted Warren Beatty's actress wife Annette Bening, who 'succeeded in capturing Hollywood's most elusive bachelor', on motherhood: 'The hardest part has been the pressure I've put on myself. You have to practise every day to free yourself of the burden of trying to be the perfect mother.'[1] Post-natal depression, for example, often results when a sense of internal inadequacy collides with society's expectations that the new mother be happy, proud, and naturally competent at loving and bringing up her baby.

Thousands (if not millions) of mothers of a previous generation who followed Truby King's advice in their sincere wish to be good parents put their infants on 4-hourly feeds, steeling themselves to withstand the heartrending cries of the babies they loved because some expert displaying a lot of confidence and the conviction of being absolutely in the right said that was the right thing to do and that this was the way to be a good parent. It is always hard to question authorities, particularly if you have never been encouraged or shown how to do so effectively. Many of these children have been in my consulting rooms as adults, reliving hours of sorrow and early decisions that there must be something wrong with them as a result of this recommended regime. Then came Dr Spock, and then his retraction. The 1960s followed, letting it all hang out with its naked dope-smoking parents and many children growing up without any discipline. They also brought in the grand and important experimental ideas of Summerhill school. I have also worked with some of these 1960s children who felt themselves permanently panic-stricken, terrified with a freedom they could not handle and absolutely abandoned by parents because there was no struc-ture or boundaries, no rules, no ideas of what was right or wrong – nothing even to rebel against!

It is hard to be a good parent under such changing fashions in expert opinions on childrearing and it has been a great comfort to many parents to give up seeking for perfection and to find competencies in just 'being good enough' – a phrase which I believe came into the field through Dr Donald Winnicott – a great paediatrician who helped many mothers and babies to find their unique ways to meet each other as separate but intimate personalities.

The scale of sexual abuse of children by their parents has recently leapt into public awareness via shocking media coverage. This kind of abuse has certainly always been com-mitted in many cultures. Freud apparently knew about it, but it seems he suppressed it, perhaps in the service of his own ambition and theories, perhaps because he just did not know what to do about it. Suddenly parents who want to become better parents, and who have been free and easy with their children, become very self-conscious. They fear whether other people, their children or spouses may see physical closeness as dangerous or seductive. I know of many men who have felt themselves become clumsy, cautious and hyper-aware of touching their daughters, so that natural spontaneous expression of affection has become stilted and self-conscious.

Children's needs and developmental stages have also been studied and written about in many different ways. Each of these makes new demands on parental competencies, often giving confusing or contradictory advice or warnings.

The proliferation of expert advice often flies in the face of the genuine personal experience of parents. For example, it used to be said that babies experience neither themselves nor their mothers as separate selves until the age of about 8 months. Most mothers would contest this on the basis of their own experiences, saying that they felt their babies saw them from shortly after birth and experienced themselves and experienced them as separate individuals virtually from the moment of being born. This has been borne out by research on human temperament, which has demonstrated quite convincingly that major temperamental factors exist pre-birth and can be identified within minutes if not hours of birth. It used to be believed that what the mother experienced during pregnancy would be transmitted to the foetus. This used to be an old wives' tale, but after decades of dismissing this as superstition it has again been found that the foetus is responsive and affected by changes in the mother's mood, her chemical and hormonal state related to stress and so on.

Wolf[2] has identified the psychological needs a parent must provide in the following paraphrased sequence. Firstly, after birth, infants need to feel merged with the care-giver, experiencing connectedness and safety. Later, infants need accurate mirroring in order to create a solid sense of themselves. This occurs when a parent reflects back to their baby its feelings, moods and actions as if they are 'in tune'. This leads to feeling appreciated for *being*, not just doing.

Wolf points out that children need to admire and idealize their parental figures. We all need powerful and protective people to look up to and emulate. Children need to feel similar (twinship) as well as different (adversarial) and oppositional on occasion without being swamped, punished or rejected. Such experiences lead to a healthy sense of self. Of course, children need to feel that they can have an impact on their care-giver. Reading the immense amount of literature prescribing all a parent needs to do and to be for their children to be healthy is daunting. No wonder parents feel hopeless and helpless as the demands for competency are so impossible to meet and difficult to establish. No wonder they sometimes just give up trying.

Reparenting and/or Rechilding

Azul found it particularly hard and demanding to be a competent father towards his baby. He had been tricked into marrying a particular woman even though he loved her, and he felt that the pregnancy too was not really his choice. Some years into psychotherapy he had just fully connected with his own childhood needs – his own desperate deprivation, the neglect by his over-worked parents and the terror of an abusive home when father came home drunk and violent towards the others. In therapy Azul had been making very good progress in learning how to become a good father to himself; but with the coming of the baby it seemed as if those rather new behaviours, feelings and attitudes about becoming a good father to himself had not quite had time to take root and become strong. His baby's crying resonated with the unclaimed crying of the child inside himself. He could never leave the house without re-experiencing in himself both the guilt his mother felt when she left the house and the dreadful abandonment which he experienced as a baby when she did so. He was so over-identified with the baby that he could hardly go to work every day without reliving his own childhood abandonment.

This type of problem has been the subject of some workshops about trying to break this vicious cycle of pseudocompetency in parents. A participant reported the following:

When I was with children I just trusted that I was not going to be persecutory or withholding with them, and that I'd know the difference. There were some times in that workshop when I didn't know what was appropriate and didn't parent, so I'd tell them I didn't know what to do – and they had better parents so we exchanged parenting skills. Anybody who says working with children is easy! – you need to be highly skilled and very well 'therapized' yourself, as it really draws on the big holes of parenting.

Parents are often pretending because they have to in response to internal and external pressure. It is only natural to be pseudocompetent if we try to meet demands on how to parent based on external demands instead of these being matched with an inner sense of confidence and trust in the Physis of every child. Physis is conceived of as the creative growth force of nature which drives development from the foetus to the adult, from illness to recovery. It is the inherent driving force of evolution. A student in regression to an earlier child state described her experience of Physis at a cellular level as 'I feel all my cells sitting up, full of spring. There's something so good in just talking about life energy.'

The following client had been doing a lot of self-development work around healing the wounds left by his own parenting, so that he was more able to give both his new baby son and the child in himself the love and protection they need and deserve:

> Client: I remember you sending me flowers before my son was born and being terribly moved by that. You were probably targeting the rough time before he was born and it was spot-on. It was the biggest and most beautiful bouquet I had ever seen; and appreciating the fullness of your gift was reparative. I have all these moments stored and can savour them again.
>
> Therapist: That is the creation of the new child inside you. That loved feeling is available to you now for all of your future life.

Many people in our Western world have been exposed, perhaps over-exposed, to the theory that early childhood trauma, neglect or bad circumstances lead to disturbed or distressed adult lives. There is, of course, a great deal of truth in this, as I hope I have amply discussed. But, as I will also show in Chapter 12, many people survive their childhoods and develop in themselves an 'invulnerable child'[3] From truly terrible roots some people create lives which are valuable, important and gratifying to themselves and others. Our childhoods and inherited bad parenting can easily and, I believe, unnecessarily become excuses. These may lead to the sins of the fathers being visited onto the nth generation; as if human beings do not also have free will and the capacity to transform not only themselves but also the worlds in which they live.

Suggestions and Exercises

- When you were just born, what did you come into the world with? How could those natural qualities be used in your life right now?
- How would you like to play with a child in a way that he or she could learn something that would be valuable in the future? Imagine yourselves playing together.
- Did you rebel against authority as a child, or did you accept it unquestioningly? Were you praised for being good when you accepted it unquestioningly?
- If you could do just one thing for a child right now, what would it be? Is it something you knew about or did as a child, or is it something born of adult experience? Is it verbal, like a piece of advice, or non-verbal, like a big hug?
- What would be one piece of advice you never had as a child, which you would have liked to have had, or found useful? Give yourself that advice now and, if possible, follow it in a way that is relevant to you now.
- Self-parenting exercise: What do you say to yourself when you are frightened, sad, angry or happy? What do you do for yourself when you are worried?
- Give your child a hug and tell him or her that you love them as loudly and energetically as you usually tell them when they have done something wrong.

CHAPTER SEVEN

Achilles in Love

THE PSEUDOCOMPETENT LOVER

Does not every decent and right-minded man love and cherish his own woman, as I loved that girl, with all my heart, though she was captive of my spear? (p. 170)

This chapter explores the surprisingly widespread phenomena of men and women who have a reputation as being good lovers, sexually attractive, or even particularly beautiful or handsome, who all feel inside themselves that they have some gruesome physical flaws or who regularly cover up for their internally sensed inadequacies in the field of love and sex. Agony columns and more serious studies by sexologists all indicate that as a culture we have become caught up in pseudocompetency in sex and love; whereas most of us still feel deeply ignorant and/or embarrassed about certain aspects of our knowledge, ability and/or performance.

Pseudocompetency also affects people deeply in terms of their intimate relationships and sexual behaviour. One of the earliest natural forms in which we see this form of pseudocompetency is in the school playground, where children may often pretend to know about sexuality and taboo topics as a way of avoiding losing face with their friends. To be smeared with 'Didn't you even know *that*?' (whatever 'that' may be) can be utterly humiliating to a young person. As I have shown in Chapter 1, somehow in our collective consciousness knowledge is connected with shame. This also connects it closely with sexuality, as in the phrase 'He had carnal knowledge of her'. It is a rare adolescent boy who has not pretended to know more about sex and sexuality, and to have done more than he has actually done, as any investigation of your male friends and acquaintances will prove.

Emotional Castration and Cover-up

A recent magazine survey questioned men on what they really know about sex. Many were confused about the basic facts regarding women's bodies and sexuality that you might have expected them to know about – and these were only the ones who answered the questionnaire.

In our society we have lost the tribal training grounds and the rites of passage which help youngsters move from a state of comparative ignorance and/or innocence to being knowledgeable and skilful as lovers or sexual partners. Some African women are taught much by the older women about the rites of courtship and sexuality in this way, such as how to do sexual exercises to improve the tone of their vaginal muscles, or how to roll their hips during intercourse so that both partners enjoy sex to the full. Of course in some Third World societies all is not so exemplary, from our Eurocentric perspective, as when 'training' has to do with destroying someone's capacity for sexual pleasure (usually women's); such as the genital mutilations of some North African tribes.[1]

According to a recent survey carried out by the Kinsey Institute more than half of participating adults gave incorrect answers to 10 out of 18 questions on sexual behaviour and contraception. In Western societies, according to the Hite Report,[2] something like 70% of women do not have fully satisfactory or orgasmic sex in their relationships. We are talking about huge numbers of women in our culture at this time, who are supposed to know about sex or are the inheritors of the sexual revolution of the 1960s and 1970s. These women are still psychologically mutilated in that they do not or cannot achieve an expectable pleasure from sharing their bodies with their partners. Of course there is a difference between psychological and actual castration. However, I believe that in terms of their capacity for genuine joy in the competent engagement with their own and other people's sexuality, my experience is that many men and women are behaving pseudocompetently and getting less from love than is possible.

The Learning Curve of Sexuality

Previous generations of course had exactly the same problem of pseudocompetency, but some people think that theirs came from not over-exposure to sex but its over-romanticizing. Older people reminisce about their glamorous screen gods and goddesses – and the fading out of the picture at the big screen kiss. All the attention was on the wooing and the chase, with the 'winning' symbolized by a lingering first kiss. Romantic comedies so often end with a big, dramatic gesture of love, or end with the couple at the altar, as if there is no life after marriage. It makes us forget that real love can often be more of an ongoing process than a single, dramatic state.

The sex and love portrayed on television is now very performance-oriented. Bodies are usually shown as perfect, young and in peak condition. This leaves a huge gap in our knowledge of true intimacy and learning to know and please one another and ourselves. And on the other hand the countervoice in our culture complains that there is too much sexual explicitness around. The fact is that the 'explicitness' is showing the seductiveness, or the athletic side of things. The basics are being left out. Huge numbers of people do not know the 'facts of life'. Many women do not know what their own vaginas look like. How may they help guide a partner in giving them pleasure if they don't know the territory themselves?

> I could never link up what I saw in the biology book with anything I knew about me or about men. That sideways diagram of all the organs cut in half . . . but I was too embarrassed to let

on that I didn't understand what this had to do with birds and bees or the disturbing feelings in my body and the way men looked at me.

So while our culture is popularly seen as sexually sophisticated and/or over-exposed to sex, this in fact makes it very difficult for people to admit that they lack basic information about themselves and their bodies, about sexuality and intimate play. We are supposed to know so much, and we actually know so little, leading to the shame to ask for and get the information. There are many people who would like to ask more about contraception but feel they have become 'too old' to be asking such basic questions, or that they will be seen as inadequate or unsophisticated in some way for not having this information.

Schools add to this fear and cover-up by the frequent inadequacy of their sex education. The bright and/or naughty kids build up a reputation for knowing a lot and if the other children want information they will go to them rather than to the books or their teachers. These precocious children may well broadcast completely false information, either out of ignorance of the truth, or sometimes spreading a rumour out of maliciousness and a sense of 'Now let them sort that one out'.

Many of us think that sexual competency is a *product* to be achieved with oneself or a partner and that, once achieved, it is possible to keep it at the same level without a continuous engagement with the cycle of learning as our partner changes, bodies change, information and curiosities change, and time changes our sexuality over the decades. With all competencies, people can become unconsciously incompetent, mechanical, boring and habituated unless they are willing to start learning over and over again the small details of their own and their partner's most intimate physical and emotional experiences.

Most long-term couples of my acquaintance, whether homosexual or heterosexual, do not have an interesting or satisfying sex life, by their own criteria. Couples also assume that other couples have busier, better sex lives or generally have more fun. It is only the sex therapists and psychotherapists who find out how many people whose friends and colleagues see them as the ideal couple have the most boring, violent or non-existent sex lives.

Think of the enormous preparation that goes into preparing for a date when you are starting a love relationship. When I suggest to couples who are complaining of a boring sex life that they set aside an evening off and cook a nice meal with candles and early bed, they say so often that sex which follows such preparation isn't spontaneous. I then ask them to remember the beginning of the relationship and how they planned their evenings – having their hair done, shopping for and preparing the meal, what they would say, what they would wear, what they would do afterwards. All this planning and scheming for seduction was anything but spontaneous!

Holden Caulfield in *The Catcher in the Rye* is an example of the pseudocompetent person's overwhelming fear of failure. His big first night with a prostitute, which he had looked forward to, eventually got him so nervous that he could only sit with the girl in his hotel room and make small talk with her – putting off the physical moment. After an evening of talking to her he then had to tell all his friends the next day that he had the best lovemaking session of his life. Prostitutes, on the other hand, often don't bluff. They are not pseudocompetent when they choose to pretend and don't feel worried about being found out, because that is their job. They may in fact be competent at pretending to feel excited and responsive – that is where their competency lies. They may develop an alternative form of currency in their sex relationships by, for example, not letting their clients kiss them.

When Sexuality Becomes Performance

The other major problem linked with this theme is people's belief that sexual competency, if we can talk about it in that way, is a kind of product, achieved once and for all in a marriage or partnership. They feel that, once two people have figured out how to do it satisfactorily for both of them, this represents competency and the same pattern over and over again just needs repeating. No wonder boredom sets in. They are not going through the natural learning cycle and accepting that, once you start to know how to do something well, it starts to habituate and become mechanical. We need to unlearn what we think we know about sexuality. This means becoming de-skilled with our partners and ourselves, so that we can continue to refresh, relearn and learn anew all aspects of sensuality, knowledge and intimacy with the other, unlearning some old habits along the way. It becomes necessary to change partners and to seek excitement in increasing artificially stimulation if there is a lack of commitment to learning and getting to know the other person yourself.

An example of avoiding the learning cycle are those people who need more and more kinkiness in order to provide stimulation instead of, or in addition to, learning more about your partner and engaging deeply in who they are as people, both in their bodies as well as their souls. The proliferation of sex manuals has indeed led to an assumption that most of us know most of what there is to know about sexuality, but my clinical and training experience has shown me that much of the time it is a pseudocompetent cover-up. A dreadful example is Linda Lovelace, star of the famous sex film 'Deep Throat', who appeared very competent in helping a man – and his friends – climax with their penises in her throat. She appeared to enjoy what was happening to her and was billed as many men's sexual goddess. Yet she tells that she was beaten every morning by her husband, put on starvation rations and systematically tortured in order to go through these performances. The film was presented as a male fantasy – the woman with the clitoris in her throat. How many women who watch that film do not feel offended, or feel that they could not admit their own discomfort? It was fashionable in the 1960s to sleep with many partners, but many people were bluffing. For many women this form of casual sex was degrading and humiliating, but they couldn't let on that they did not know how to say no. Many were embarrassed about being virgins and so had their first experiences without the preparation and education which would have made their sexuality much more important and precious to them.

A sexually active and attractive man finally goes to bed with the girl he has been chasing for weeks – and suddenly finds that, after all the anticipation and the enjoyment of the 'chase', he cannot get an erection. To his shame, he realizes that sex has been something he has done up to now with people he has not particularly cared for. He can flirt and be charming and sexy with anyone except the one person he really values and cares for. Impotence has just never figured in his life except as something to joke about in other people. He feels he cannot talk about it to anyone, least of all the close male friends with whom he used to share those jokes. Another young man carefully cuts the size labels out of his underpants in case his girlfriend should see they say 'Small'. Sex is also a powerful shaming tool; in the Second World War the airmen dropped boxes of condoms marked 'small' over enemy lines as a blatant act of male humiliation.

Young Adonises, or women with a reputation as beautiful sex goddesses, can often turn out to be very shy or even call themselves 'frigid'. Some men and women, whether gay or not, have become so involved in the vanity of physical appearance that they are unwilling to risk the competency of looking beautiful or sexy for the smeared lipstick or the unwashed face of the genuinely passionate encounter. In conversation, flirting with a heavy sexual innuendo may also cover up a fear of having to engage mentally as well as sexually with a partner. People may be far more anxious about talking to their new partner than going to bed with them, so that the idea of conversation over the dinner table on their date becomes terrifying. Will she think I'm boring? Will he expect me to have an opinion on everything? Heavy sexual innuendo stops the conversation ever becoming 'serious', so sex or at least the promise of great sex becomes the currency of the relationship instead of friendship, companionship or enjoyable conversation.

Vaclav goes out one evening with a group of friends, from work and elsewhere, and he invites his old friend Marina along. For most of the evening Vaclav and Marina talk and dance together, sometimes putting an arm around each other. They have privately both acknowledged a mutual affection but they have no sexual involvement, as both are committed in other relationships and Vaclav will soon be leaving the country. Next day Abbie, a work colleague, says knowingly and in typical male fashion: 'You got on alright with Marina then?' and 'I didn't know you knew her so well', implying that Vaclav has a way with the ladies.

Vaclav explains that they are just good friends, which Abbie clearly does not believe; but he does not push the point, partly because he is also unsure which way the relationship will develop and partly because he is secretly flattered by Abbie's view of him. Vaclav and Marina maintain their friendship. Other people echo Abbie: 'Lucky bastard!' and 'You're a dark horse – hope your wife doesn't find out!' Vaclav feels trapped. He is struggling between various pseudocompetencies; the pressure from macho colleagues to imply that he is sleeping with a beautiful woman when he is not; the pressure from his social group to ignore the situation which automatically implies that he is deceiving his wife; the fact that he is telling the truth but not being believed; and his internal reality that people believing he has a beautiful, intelligent girlfriend makes him feel good and respected.

The Level of Choicefulness or Awareness

There is an assumption in our society that human relationships are natural, and that everyone should know how to communicate, how to deal with failure, to make friends, to invite someone to a party. Women's magazines are full of questions from girls and women about whether or not to kiss on the first date or when is the 'right' time in a new relationship to go to bed together, and not all are from young women. Many other women are re-entering the dating arena after bereavement or break-up. Inside these people and others experience great anxiety, often fearing a party more than enjoying or taking pleasure in it, in anxiety about being found out because they are basically socially incompetent. This is far more widespread than I would ever have imagined.

I have noticed that many people will admit privately or in the consulting room that they are pretending most of the time to be socially able or skilful, whereas they experience tremendous anxiety before social occasions and a similar kind of strain and exhaustion afterwards that I have described elsewhere, in public speaking or other areas of competency.

Social Anxiety

Several people have wanted to learn social competency as part of their therapy. Much of counselling and psychotherapy is providing a trusting relationship and permissive atmosphere, which allows people to admit these things they don't know. On social occasions such as parties there can be a sense of being 'nowhere to hide' if you are shy or pseudo-competent, but it is important to remember that one can circulate if feeling stuck. Some people are helped by very simple tips, such as if you feel uncomfortable at the party, hand around the snacks or the drinks tray. For example, one highly skilled and competent therapist in session with me was struggling with how to feel more comfortable at social gatherings. He thought a good thing to do was identify another person who is lonely or on their own, and to go and talk to them. But this, of course, is often not best because you then get two introverted, shy people standing struggling together. Often it is best to join a three- or foursome or the liveliest corner of the room, and it is then much easier to enter the conversation in a diluted way. One is therefore less exposed, and slightly more supported. However, many of these people would not be seen dead reading a book on conversational skills. In the same way some people would not like their friends or partners to see that they are looking at a book on the joy of sex, in case people thought they did not know what they were doing. So the pretence and the unquenched desire to know are perpetuated.

Addiction to Pseudocompetency

The American 'recovery movement' suggests that you admit you are addicted to sex, alcohol, drugs, other addictions. A mass market of literature on addiction, co-dependency and recovery has been created, and it tells us that one of the first steps to recovery is to give up denial. Being addicted to pseudocompetency means you are in denial that there is any kind of problem or unhappiness in the first place. Once you can admit that you don't know or fear something, you can begin to get the help you need – not only in that one issue you are pseudocompetent about but also in learning about learning, about how to manage ignorance, incompetence and competence, and how to manage them all your life.

In our culture where 'being in the know' is important, it is not valuable to be someone who is learning, it is only valuable to be someone who 'has the knowledge'. Unless teachers are willing to show their own learning processes, the myth will be perpetuated. It is essential to see how your teachers learn and cope with varying degrees of competency and incompetency. A senior sex therapist said she did not need to go to sessions to explore her own partnership, because she knew it all and did not need it. It was only people in trouble who sought that sort of help. The same aura has surrounded counselling and psychotherapy and it is only recently beginning to lift. People are now beginning to accept that they may seek counselling for self-development and enhancement, not just because they have deep problems.

Exploration or Advice

There used to be a sad and inaccurate division between exploratory and prescriptive (advising) counselling/psychotherapy. This led to a particular kind of pseudocompetency among professionals who did not investigate whether or not it is appropriate to teach somebody something. Instead, they always assumed that people either knew or could find out, because they had become so pedantic about not rescuing people. The client says she does not know what to do. The therapist answers: 'Are you asking me to help you?' or 'You can find this out for yourself.' Counselling and psychotherapy can be over-precious about not giving affective education in how to handle emotions, when people may genuinely be needing the information. For example, one man came to a therapist feeling very guilty, self-punishing and self-blaming because, although happily married, he occasionally masturbated. He saw this as a sign of immaturity and was ashamed to admit it to anybody. He was tormenting himself with this 'evidence' of his inadequacy and immaturity as a man.

Taking an exploratory approach in this case means we could explore why it was hard for him to accept this, how it was related to his childhood, what fantasies he had about his therapist, and so on through reams of material. The client would in fact have been much more helped and benefited by much more straightforward information. In this particular case the therapist asked if he knew the incidence of masturbation amongst married men, because in the client's view it was always abnormal and therefore sick or immature. He did not know of any other married men who masturbated. The therapist asked him if he'd discussed it with his friends and, of course, the client replied that this was the last thing anyone would want to talk about because it would show you up as a baby, as dirty, or that you were not getting enough sex. Having established that he was genuinely ignorant, the therapist then quoted from and then gave him some books, including the now rather old-fashioned Kinsey Report, which clearly state that most married men masturbate quite regularly. In other words, it is statistically quite normal and no reflection on their partners, or necessarily a criticism of their marriage if they should do so. The client was immediately much relieved and this simple piece of information made a lasting and beneficial change both to his self-esteem and to his relationship with his wife, because he no longer felt guilty, abnormal or inadequate. Neither was he covering up any more.

'I Want What I'm Giving You'

One of the commonest sources of human misunderstanding is our tendency to give others what we want rather than to give them what they want. The biggest confusion seems to be a distortion of love between how I want to be loved and how you want to be loved. In the simplest terms, Lizzie likes to be hugged and cuddled and taken to bed when she's upset, and Ben likes to be distracted and taken out for a meal or a movie. When Ben finds Lizzie upset, he takes her out to distract her and cannot understand why she is not delighted with his attempts to amuse and entertain her. On the other hand, when Ben is upset, Lizzie feels puzzled and alienated when he does not respond to her nurturing and caretaking offers to put him to bed and bring him dinner there. The variations of misunderstandings on this theme are enormous. 'I like surprise parties so I'll give you one', not thinking (or believing) that you can be so different from me that you hate surprise parties and find them a strain (even though you've told me this before!).

Similarly, we often buy our friends and partners the gifts that we really want ourselves, and then feel offended when they do not seem as delighted as we would naturally be to receive them. Despite our real affection for the person we give to, we often do not take their personal style or taste into account. Another common variation on this tendency is to give the person what we think they want. We all know a person who gets a reputation for collecting some object, say model ships or china pigs. We automatically buy them a model ship or a china pig for every occasion. Even if the object is hideous, we buy it for its own sake and assume our friend must be pleased, and when visiting we look out for our own contribution among his rows and rows of ornaments. Our friend may or may not have the courage and honesty to say 'Enough is enough! I'll make my own collection because the *choosing* is what gives me pleasure!'

Pseudocompetent lovers may only be able to give the love that they want to have. This is a case for the importance of celebrating difference, modifying the drawbacks of our virtues, but cherishing the qualities in our partners which, by their very otherness, become the fulcrum for greatest attraction and most significant mutual transformation.

I have found from many years' work as a couples therapist that there are three main categories of difference for couples. These are (a) unacceptable behaviour (b) negotiable issues and (c) unchangeable aspects of self. Sorting the changes you desire into these different categories means that each partner can then focus on more realistically achievable goals.

The first category concerns areas of unacceptable behaviour: in other words: 'This is what I won't accept from you.' It is behaviour of the other person that is essentially non-negotiable, concerning the basic human needs for security, economic well-being, a sense of belonging, recognition and control over one's own life. The second category, negotiable issues, is the area of 'This is what I do or don't want you to do, and this is what you do or don't want me to do.' It is this second area in which most couples can work most effectively towards understanding, improving and even transforming their relationship. Once a couple are clear about what is and what is not acceptable as pre-requirements, or what would constitute grounds for an irretrievable breakdown, then they can begin to deal with the differences which they can, and may be willing to, change. The third category, unchangeable aspects, is no longer about attitudes or behaviour, but about selfhood. It concerns those aspects of the self which are essentially unchangeable, or very hard to change without injury to one's own integrity as a person. It is about one's fundamental temperament, constitution or personality: 'This is who I am. This is who you are.' For each long-term loving partner in a couple it is essential to separate out the changes in attitude and behaviour which may be necessary or desirable, from changes in the essential quality of a person which would make them very different from the person you love.

I will end this chapter with a story about love and wisdom. A seeker went to a Zen master to learn to love. The master agreed and told him to go away for 7 years and love a stone. After 7 years the disciple returned and told the master that he had now achieved pure love for the stone. The master sent him off to love a tree for the next 7 years. This the disciple did, and returned after 7 years to report his love for the tree. The master sent him off to love a mountain for the next 7 years, and the disciple returned after his 7 years to tell of his love for the mountain. 'Now,' said the master, 'You may be ready to love another person.'

Suggestions and Exercises

- What are the books you would not like to be seen on your bedside table? And who would you least like to see them?
- Remember: every time you have your heart broken it gets practice in healing itself again.
- Make a list of the presents you would really like to receive, and make a list of the presents your partner would like to receive. If you don't know, find out. Notice differences and similarities between these. Write down what you need from your partner when you are ill, stressed or distressed. Write down what your partner needs in the same circumstances, and if you don't know, find out.
- Remember that the qualities of our partners which first made us fall in love with them are the essential qualities of that person. It is unfair, and probably impossible, to try and change them because even if you did succeed, they would

end up being a different person from the one you originally found attractive.

- Learn how to settle differences creatively. You may want to sound off for quite a long time before you feel better or are willing to accept reparation. Your partner may be able to let go of a hurt or resentment quite easily and differently from you.
- Fill in your own examples of unacceptable behaviour, negotiable issues and unchangeable aspects of self on the following worksheet, and get your partner to do the same on a separate copy. Spend time learning from one another what your views of each category are, and start on negotiating the issues that can be changed. People can differ surprisingly on these issues.

Unacceptable behaviour	'This is what I won't accept from you'	
Negotiable issues	'This is what I do or don't want you to do'	
Unchangeable	'This is who I am' aspects of self	

- Never stop learning about sex, reading about sex, discovering your own sexuality, going on relationship enrichment workshops, making time to be sensual together, massaging each other. Sexuality withers when it is not tended.
- Do not expect your partner to be your counsellor or psychotherapist. They will always fail because they cannot possibly make up to you what went wrong for you in the past then – and vice versa, you cannot, even if you want to, make up for their own past. We can nurture, care for and love each other as the mature people we have become in the here and now, with the fondness and care for the child within each of us, but we cannot be one another's soul doctors. Even medical doctors know that they cannot be both ethical and useful in operating on their family. Learn your lover's language. It is highly likely for any couple that one of you lives on a martial planet, for example called Mars, and the other on a planet symbolically called Venus. The languages, the norms, the bodies and the feelings are very different. You may never truly understand why someone would want to do things in a particular way rather than your way. True love means that we can tolerate and celebrate another person's different world, even though we may never be able truly to understand it in the way that they do.
- Remember that love is not just about loving one other person in a romantic way. It is also about loving one's work, one's family, life itself.

CHAPTER EIGHT

Achilles as Healer

THE PSEUDOCOMPETENT COUNSELLOR OR PSYCHO-THERAPIST

At least you can rescue me . . . They say you have some excellent prescriptions that you learnt from Achilles, who was taught by Chiron, the civilized Centaur. (p. 219)

As we saw in Chapter 1, Achilles was famous as a healer, despite the fact that he was also a great warrior. He cured as well as inflicting wounds. He treated Telephus' spear wound by scraping some rust from his spear into it, using the ancient homeopathic principle that 'like cures like'. In counselling and psychotherapy, people often experience the pain of their wounds more intensely before they get well. Achilles also used the herb 'achilleos' which he had discovered.

Counsellors and psychotherapists (as well as others in the so-called helping professions) are included here as our modern healers and carers of the soul. This chapter is based on a great deal of experience of training and supervising counsellors, psychotherapists and supervisors, and their supervisors and trainers. It grew from my engagement with the frequently occurring pseudocompetency issues which affect them.

Entry into the Profession

Pseudocompetency in healing has to do with our childhood roots. Many people choose to become counsellors or psychotherapists because they were the psychologically precocious children in their family. As youngsters they intuitively got involved with understanding and trying to help the pain and distress of a disturbed or limited childhood home. Often they were so-called 'care-taker' children, and they became inappropriately the confidante of a parent or they were eldest siblings taking care of the others in a dysfunctional family. Such early training and experience in the world of disturbed and disturbing feelings can create an appetite for tending wounds. This intuitive talent makes them initially suitable as counsellors and psychotherapists. But it is based on the failed attempt of the child within them to cure the damaged family of their own origin. Of course they also have the ability to inflict wounds on both themselves and others. So, there are frequently problems which arise later in training, in supervision, towards examination qualifications, or even subsequent to developing a great reputation which need very careful identification and management.

According to a very famous psychotherapist, Ferenczi, all children have a compulsive desire to heal their families. Searles said that one of the most powerful innate strivings from infancy is a wish to be therapeutic or to cure our fellow human beings. Childhood trauma can lead to a precocious maturity which is a result of copying or identification with admired others rather than the result of a thorough integration and working through for oneself.

One of my first analysts told me that he thought there was only one kind of person that came into our profession. He said it was those who were wounded in some important way and who were trying to heal themselves in trying to help others. He went on to say that there were two kinds of people who remained in the profession: those who resolve their problems and those who do not. In some ways this is true.

However, this may lead to the false idea that counsellors or psychotherapists should be perfect individuals who have resolved all their personal issues and who are untouched by the stresses, challenges and upsets of life. Of course this is not the case. Training in counselling and psychotherapy should never make us immune to the pain, the confusion and the intricacies of our human existence. Hopefully it can but put us in a better position to deal with ourselves and others from some measure of wisdom, compassion and understanding. Self-knowledge is not an inoculation against life. Only counsellors and psychotherapists who are still engaged in the struggle to become more human can empathize from their own experience with the pain and confusion of others.

The idea of the *wounded healer* has been around perhaps as long as human beings have been engaged in the art of healing. However, this should not be an excuse for counsellors to 'bleed' all over their clients. The journey towards becoming a counsellor or psychotherapist and remaining fruitfully active in this difficult profession must be accompanied by constant soul-searching and disciplined controlling of the borders between one's own problems and difficulties and those of the people we serve. To this end, most people remain in personal therapy and supervision for most of their professional lives.

The notion of the wounded healer can easily lead to pseudocompetence or sustain pseudocompetence. If the ideal is to be perfect oneself, of course we must always fail – and indeed should fail. A restless striving for a mythical state of perfection must inevitably lead to an alienation from the human condition and thus from the capacity to be helpful. However, there do need to be criteria for what is good enough, and many counsellors and psychotherapists are unclear and confused about these. This kind of doubt and lack of accurate calibration is indeed a sign of pseudocompetency. Supervisors and trainers should always take such concerns very seriously until the counsellor or psychotherapist can be reasonably trusting of a reliable 'inner supervisor'.

Training in the 'Impossible Profession'

It is important to remember that formal education like school or university is often structured in terms of consecutive years, but this does not reflect accurately where people are in their own learning process. As a teacher in this profession, I remain open to the idea that people will be using me at different levels, depending upon where they want to pitch themselves and at what stage they are. Each trainee has to find out how to use their teacher, how to make the most of the desire and impetus to learn that is within each of them. The same is true of training trainees and supervisors:

> I was asked to be an examiner. I was flattered to be asked, because I really wanted to be an examiner, but knew that I didn't really know what questions to ask. I did go and find out, but I still don't know enough. I asked to sit in on an exam, so I'd know what was expected. Next time I am going to make sure I know enough, and when I am asked again, I will say yes. I am pleased that I took the initiative to do that.

One trainee summarized his recent session with a client in terms of success or failure in the following metaphor: 'My intervention was brilliant – but the client still died.' Another admitted just how deep her feelings of pseudocompetency were:

> At some level I'm going to come unstuck. My fantasy is people finding out I'm no good. Not only about not knowing, but about my innate ability and talent as a human being. Even as I say that I tell myself that it can be sorted out by training, but I feel there's some contamination in there. Even when I'm doing my work properly, I struggle to stay an adult. I want to do it well, but to be a responsible adult. I feel like a precocious kid pretending to be able to drive a car.

When trainees show great anxiety about coming up to standard for exams, you know they are not up to standard because they have not fully developed their judgement about how to assess their own competency against the criteria acceptable for the professional. Competency always includes knowing what is *good enough*.

When teaching counsellors or therapists I find that at a certain stage they often say that they feel more vulnerable and unskilful now than they used to at the beginning of their training – yet they know more now. They have learnt a lot of theory and done many hours of practical work, as well as being in ongoing personal psychotherapy, but they will start to think: 'Am I sure I can manage this?' with a new urgency. They talk about feeling deskilled, of unlearning and relearning. They each find out for themselves that the more you know and learn, the more stupid you can feel about how you managed in the past. I teach them and/or they find out that it's a natural stage in the developmental cycle. In fact, if you feel confused, de-skilled and clumsy, you may be in an accelerated learning period. This is of course not confined to the acknowledged 'beginners'. A senior supervisor told me:

> If a supervisee asks me a question that I don't know the answer to, I feel in my head that I should know. I know that I don't have to have all the answers, all the theory, but I feel I have to.

We each usually teach in the way that we want to be taught, just as we often give the presents we would like to receive. Our styles may be very different. The go-ahead type will urge the students to 'have a go', which may leave them feeling unsupported or lacking theory. The people who encourage dependency will overvalue the 'holding' environment. The way we teach our trainees will also form the basis for their own working style in future. The facts have been well researched and documented which prove that new supervisors tend to supervise in the way they were previously supervised. It is easy for both trainers and trainees to make dogma of things we either do not understand or have skimped on the fundamental principles. It is also easy for trainees to respond not to the principles themselves but to the charisma of the teacher. Dogma can lose all the freshness of the original idea or creativity ethic. Training therefore requires that we work to unlearn earlier introjected working styles, and develop our own individual style. For example, it was thought for many years that supervision should be done in the manner of the relevant counselling system. However, many counselling supervisors now use an integrative approach to supervision, meaning that they will draw from a variety of approaches and techniques and apply them as appropriate.

As a healer of others, sometimes you need to be an anchor for them. If they meet you head-on with a very high energy, your job may be to meet it, steady it, de-escalate it and then help them channel it as appropriate. Another task is to provide a safe arena for people in which they can vent the anger that has not been expressed in acting out their destructive feelings. The force of the emotions that come up may be frightening or seem dangerous, both for the client and for the counsellor. We need to be careful to build appropriate boundaries, to keep the safety for ourselves, and to develop an appropriate relationship with each of our trainees. We need to be competent to deal with very strong feelings of anger as well as very strong feelings of love.

How ignorant the experts are on the whole, and how important it is that they get in touch with what they are ignorant about, so they don't import or broadcast further incompetence, such as those helping professionals who know they are good at their job but have become incompetent in the social field.

It is vital that experienced trainers continue to build new self-development opportunities and challenges into their training situation to stretch and extend themselves. This will prevent the staleness that undermines and drains many previously excellent trainers, leaving them bored and disillusioned with their work or again, unconsciously incompetent as in the beginning of the cycle. Habitual mannerisms and 'hardening of the categories' are possible pitfalls for the experienced trainers with their increase in confidence and their unselfconscious skill.

Good teachers enhance and confirm the worth of all participants ('I feel more intelligent and more gifted when I'm with my trainer'), without diminishing their own excellence through false modesty. Problematic teachers elevate themselves at the cost of group members; who may end up feeling inadequate contrasted to the trainer. Experienced trainers with a good reputation benefit from the halo effect – the positive anticipation that the 'great teacher' will do 'great teaching or supervision'. However, they also suffer from the 'pedestal effect' – the frequent human desire to find or invent feet of clay, which can preoccupy trainees at the expense of their own learning.

Supervision

Psychotherapy is a particularly difficult profession in which to achieve a good match between externally assessed competence and subjective confidence. It is a very private, almost invisible and subtle activity to which supervisors and trainers rarely have direct access except in conjoint working or through the use of audio- or video-tape. However, even though it may be mysterious in some ways, it should not be mystified. Both clients and counsellors have the right and responsibility to share information in a responsible and empowering way. Obviously supervision is one of the primary avenues to insure against incompetency and establish reliable criteria and performance as a good-enough psychotherapist. Supervisors need to be on the alert for all the many ways in which trainees both may ask for all their cover-ups to be exposed as well as they may be hiding some of their uncertainties or errors from fear of being shamed, rather than understood and helped.

I would plead that people never apply the term 'pseudo-competency' as a diagnosis to a trainee or a supervisee; but be alert to someone responding to a description of the syndrome in an abstract or theoretical way, or teach the criteria for identifying areas of pseudocompetency in oneself. Be careful and compassionate when people open up this very private area of themselves for discussion – they could easily feel ashamed or humiliated, thus perhaps recreating a similar trauma to that which led to the problem in the first place. It may be important to work with this person in private before they rejoin the group. Welcome this kind of self-investigation as if it is a normal part of learning for everybody, and raise realistic hopes that deficits that have been covered up for many years can be identified, dealt with and repaired without a person being labelled as 'pathological', 'sick', 'deceitful' or 'irrational'.

Experienced supervisors need to work with a range of supervisees so that they gain experience across a wide spectrum. It is important that they continue to supervise beginning counsellors so that they retain their appreciation of the beginner's process. At the outset of this new stage of training, it may be important for trainee supervisors to give up their previous frames of reference and develop what we call *beginner's mind* – empty of previous assumptions and set patterns of working. I have personally found it useful at intervals to recreate such conditions by learning new and apparently unrelated skills such as Tai Chi. 'Beginner's mind' assists experienced supervisors to sharpen their empathy for the learner. The more experienced the supervisor, the more important it may be for them to find situations where they 'worry' (again or for the first time) about what 'the teacher' may think of them, where they experience the characteristic jerkiness of the learning process and the excruciating self-consciousness of those first risks and clumsy mistakes as well as the burgeoning sense of challenge and achievement in the perhaps small moments of early achievement.

As discussed in Chapter 3, the natural learning cycle never ends, for everything is constantly evolving. Learning is not always pleasant. One trainee told me:

> The longer I am in therapy, the more my friends keep dropping away. It is a painful realization, that my needs will not be met in my doing arena – and they shouldn't be. Our being needs and our doing needs must be met in different arenas. It's like drinking from an empty trough with barbed wire round it.

As soon as one cycle is completed, another begins. The urge to learn is not a compulsive, externally motivated search for mystical perfection, it is more a natural organismic urge to grow and develop and to become more skilled, more understanding and more compassionate. Being in touch with this evolutionary drive in ourselves enables trainers of trainers and supervisors to experience, model and inspire their charges in similar ways.

There is plenty of research to prove that training in the different approaches to psychotherapy does not make their senior practitioners any more or less effective in the eyes of the client than senior people in any other discipline. To test this, I asked some of my own clients what had been the most significant parts of their own change. The replies were many and varied: 'That book you recommended'; 'The time you were happy to see me'; 'The time you said such and such a thing . . .'. It was like the gardener doing everything he could think of to help a plant grow and then asking the healthy plant what went right. The plant would probably tell him it was that ray of sunlight that came just at the right angle and moment. At an international conference of integrative psychotherapists, an approach was discussed which involved doing a few sessions of one school of therapy and then a few of another approach, and then integrate both. Someone in the audience pointed out that it is usually the client who *actually* does the integrating – paying attention to some things, ignoring others, embroidering, censoring or amplifying in their own way, potentially independently of what the counsellor is doing.

The Unfair Expectations of Others, or the Need for Kings and Queens

There is an old superstition that doctors should never get ill. If you are a psychologist, there can be the danger that people expect you to have all the answers, never to have the equivalent of psychological flu, problems or doubts. A

pseudocompetent expectation of psychotherapists or counsellors being without a human flaw also breeds
pseudocompetency in others. As we have seen, the most
important thing in learning is learning how to learn. Seeking
perfection does not help; we need practical help in how to set
up the steps towards improvement. It is a natural human
need to have a teacher who has sorted it all out – the psychological equivalent of a perfect parent, a king or a queen. In
fact in the twentieth century many of the ideological heroes
have been tarnished – Freud, Marx, monarchies. What we
need is to find a way of valuing the teachers of ignorance or
of the learning process, rather than the teachers of knowledge
per se. When people need bread, you can give them bread *or*
you can teach them how to grow corn and to bake bread.
Should we solve people's problems or teach them how to
solve problems?

Growing is about a willingness to take teaching from any
source, to be flexible and open in your own learning. We need
not expect to learn only from institutions and textbooks, but
need to listen to the experiences of others and find through
this what works best for ourselves. Knowledge is not incre-
mental, in that you learn more and more and more. Instead
you learn things and let go of them.

A senior trainer told me:

> I used to think that a good training seminar would have no
> conflict or disagreement within it. Now I have a different kind
> of competency. I know I can still train at the point where I run
> out of knowing what to do, at the point where our knowledge
> breaks down, and still know how to help people when every-
> thing they know has broken down. This is one of the most
> important teaching competencies.

The Loneliness of the Long-distance Psychotherapist

One of the most important ways in which I have found that
counsellors and psychotherapists are pseudocompetent is in
terms of looking after themselves. Because of their desire to

help and their preoccupation with the needs of others, they easily become negligent of their own – particularly if they have had inadequate parenting about self-care during child-hood. As counsellors and psychotherapists it is therefore vital that we get our satisfactions, excitements, our eroticism and intimacy from people in our personal, family or friend-ship circle rather than from our relationships with clients or patients. Working in the helping professions is extremely demanding because you are using yourself as an instrument. Usually it needs loving care and nourishment. Sometimes that self may get out of tune or need a massive overhaul.

Doctors and psychotherapists have a very high suicide rate. In a profession which is this invisible, the strain of pseudocompetency and the fear of being found out can be incapacitating in the long term. Even when there are not early psychological roots, the long-term demands on the person of the helper in the caring professions can be exhausting, de-moralizing and debilitating. Even though one's training as a doctor, social worker, counsellor or voluntary worker may be adequate and one's own confidence and competence well matched, people in these professions are rarely properly equipped to prevent burn-out. Burn-out happens when pro-fessionals or voluntary workers lose their involvement with the people with whom they are working to an unhealthy degree. Often they are physically and emotionally ex-hausted, yet they may continue working beyond the point when they experience respect and positive feelings for their clients. There may also be a loss of creativity and enthusiasm for the work, drug dependence, depression and an increase of physical disease. It is my belief that burn-out is often aggravated if not substantially caused by the strain of pseudocompetency in professionals who have to confidently cope with circumstances way beyond their competence – for example, hospital closures, resource cut-backs, psychiatric neglect, able-bodied and cultural prejudice, and so on.

Freud was once asked by a journalist what were for him the two most important aspects of life. He answered: 'To love and to work.' In the caring professions they can often ethically and creatively co-exist. Discovering and celebrating the fluctuating rhythm between them may, however, take a lifetime.

Suggestions and Exercises

• List three reasons why you want to be a counsellor or psychotherapist. Berne[1] suggested that beginning counsellors do this. Then list another two reasons. It is often the case that the latter two contain the most authentic and honest reasons. Discuss these with your supervisor if appropriate.

If You Are a Psychotherapist or Counsellor

• Have you ever been scared of not being able to help a client? Is it your own fear, or partly the client's expectation if he or she had pseudocompetent parents?
• Have you felt that you are the only person who could help a particular client? Do you need to let go of the desire to heal?
• Are you romanticizing or devaluing the archetypal image of the wounded healer in your life?
• Make a list of the questions that you are frightened or ashamed to ask about the theory, ethics or practice of your work in the caring professions. Find a person (trainer, supervisor or colleague) and make the opportunity to ask these questions and to clarify any confusion you feel.
• *Burn-out checklist*

Enthusiasm for your work	Boredom or despair
A feeling of vitality and aliveness at work	Exhaustion or numbness
Eager anticipation of challenge	Avoidance and fear of 'another difficult situation'

| Adequate support and a sense of value | Lack of support and a sense of futility |
| Working competently and well | Working harder and harder with less and less effect |

Your spontaneous responses to this set of polarities may indicate how much you need to re-evaluate your professional choice, your current level of resources and your plans for a satisfying and exciting future.

If You Are a Trainer or a Supervisor

• Move carefully with your students – give them time; avoid them hurrying up to solve the problem or to grow up and skip parts of it. Stay with them in the despair of not knowing for a while rather than hurrying them into thinking. Being allowed to show their vulnerability may heal the need to make a secret of it. Welcoming their requests to ask questions about the basic things ('What I am supposed to know already') can help to heal the shame. Be extremely cautious about reassurance and support – make sure that is what is needed rather than questioning and education. Be alert to cries for help underneath self-doubt or bravado.

CHAPTER NINE

Achilles the Artist

THE RELATIONSHIP BETWEEN THE SECRET FLAW AND CREATIVITY

With that, Achilles held out his arms to clasp the spirit, but in vain. It vanished like a wisp of smoke and went gibbering underground.
(p. 414)

In this chapter I explore and develop the relationship between the secret flaw of the Achilles Syndrome and creativity. There are discussions of the creation process, using examples from artists' lives, and case studies, and we see how, by learning from their natural creative cycles, they apply this successfully. The particular role of Physis as a creative urge is also explored.

Creativity

Creativity is the capacity to produce new inventions, ideas, objects or artistic performances. Usually we think of creativity in terms of something new or original, but in some sense, the sun is new each day. Creativity is also about the novelty and originality of arranging existing material or ideas in new or unusual patterns, and having them accepted as being of some value, whether to yourself or to others.

Feeling and behaving incompetently seems always to be a vital part of learning new skills, and it is an unavoidable part of the creative process. This is why one of the ways of breaking pseudocompetency is to develop genuine creativity. Creative activity allows incompetence to emerge, for it is to do with experimentation, play, building up and knocking down. Feelings of incompetence always accompany genuine creative endeavour, where one faces a blank canvas or empty sheet, because in the creative life one is doing something that nobody else has done before. As we have seen in earlier chapters, we should feel able to acknowledge incompetence if we have never done a particular activity at that level before. In truth, creativity exists purely as itself and as a form of self-expression, so cannot be fully judged in terms of competence or incompetence. But only by fully coming up against his or her incompetence does the artist or practitioner become more competent.

Everybody is creative to some extent, and creativity is not restricted to the more usual art forms. All of us as children and adults have experienced moments of inventing new and exciting things, only to discover later that someone had already done that. The fact that someone else has done this in no way makes the product of the child or the adult less creative. Creativity has to do with cooking, bringing up children, writing letters to friends, picking good presents, solving international peace problems, thinking up marketing strategies, etc. Creativity colours every field of human endeavour. So in this chapter I am emphasizing artistic life process as opposed to the competency-based life choices. This is done in order to highlight the extremes. In studying the life patterns of people who have dedicated themselves to art and creativity we can indeed learn more about the process in ourselves. In this way we can find our creativity more and more in our everyday actions, from the way we put on make-up to the rituals of a tribal dance.

If you try and avoid the incompetency part of the cycle of learning you cannot become truly competent. A painter friend said to me:

'I can't get past the initial stage when I start painting again after a long break; I can't persevere, I'm too impatient to go through this stage of mistakes before eventually creating good paintings.'

We have a popular idea of the artist as mad or the genius as absent-minded. Sometimes this is true. However, many great artists were not more or less mad in any way than anybody else in the population, and the proportion of artists who become psychotic or suicides is probably less than the proportion of doctors or psychotherapists who go mad or commit suicide. In terms of our Western culture we have also been unfortunate in that Freud, although a very creative person himself, thought that creativity in adults is a form of the more primitive drives of sex (Eros) and aggression (Thanatos). For Freud, as for many ordinary people, there was thus a connection between creativity and the abnormal. For example, in his important book on creativity, Storr[1] points out that if the author had experienced for himself or seen a baby playing in a bath with the shifting, flashing water shining in the sun there would be no need for the Freudian interpretation that Leonardo da Vinci's interest and artistic flair stemmed from him suffering enuresis as a child.

Jung suggested the symbol or archetype of the animus and anima; the anima being the female counterpart of the male which he carries within him, and the animus being the male inner counterpart of the female. The artist is often encouraged to get in touch with his anima, the muse, inspiration and guidance. It has been a traditionally male province. Female artists are therefore encouraged now to bring into awareness the strength and power of their animus, remembering its enormous power to destroy as well as create. However creative or otherwise we may be, we should never marry our muse, for doing so starts to externalize the power within onto an external figure, and we come to expect the external mate to substitute for the inner mate. Our job in creative endeavour is to mate with our own creativity.

Physis, the Creative Life Force

I believe that creativity is the third independent and important drive in our lives, called Physis. Physis is different from

Table 9.1 *Characteristics of the three drives – Thanatos, Eros and Physis*[a]

Tizanatos	Eros	Physis
death	survival	life
death instinct	sexual instinct	pleasure instinct
destruction	procreation	creation/creativity
self-destruction	self-preservation	self-transformation
seeks freedom	seeks	seeks fulfilment/
from striving	gratification	realization
ending	beginning	evolving
expiration	inspiration	aspiration

[a] Thanatos, the death instinct, is also called 'mortido' and it is inwardly directed. Eros, being the libido, is outwardly directed. Physis however integrates both directions, for it is inwardly and outwardly directed.

the death or survival instincts in a number of different ways as I show in Table 9.1.

Physis is a generalized creative force of nature. It is the healing factor in illness, the energetic motive for evolution and the driving force of creativity in the individual and collective psyche. Physis can be understood as the life force or élan vital. It underlies all therapy, all life. It precedes Eros and Thanatos and operates at a cellular level, maybe even a planetary level. It carries with it an inherent tendency for transformation. Physis is symbolized in the one that tells the story, who makes meaning, even if we can't always see the meaning too well, for as Aristotle said: 'Physis loves to hide.' When we try to clasp the spirit of creativity too tightly, it goes 'gibbering underground'. We all have times when we feel that Physis is hiding, at the times when we are not in touch with our life force. We lose touch with the green shoots, with the urge to move on and out in new growth, to evolve.

Inner Motivation Versus Outer Motivation

In counselling psychotherapy and consultancy we discover over and over again that as clients or organizations get closer to their true self or 'first nature', they connect more with an inner healing or creative drive. This brings a growing awareness and appreciation of universal meanings – striving towards connectedness with spiritual, religious or transcendental values.

I think there is incompatibility between pseudocompetency and creativity, in the same way that it is impossible to feel relaxed and anxious at the same time. Of course we are seeing that neither creativity nor pseudocompetency are permanent states. They may come and go over time, last for very short periods or a lifetime. I believe truly creative people are drawing their energy from the creative drive inside themselves. They are not usually performing to meet some external demand. They are speaking from the inside out.

In fact it is almost characteristic of creativity that it is often rebellious against externally set standards or popular ideas. Artists tend to rebel; to do things which people disapprove of, or shock the establishment, whereas pseudocompetents often tend to comply, trying to please the establishment and get its approval or reward, or fear abandonment or rejection by the agreed establishment. Pseudocompetents fear unpopularity, being embarrassed, being 'found out'. Truly creative, ground-breaking artists are almost inevitably rejected by people in their immediate vicinity or the people of their time. The famous examples come to mind are that Picasso couldn't draw, that Chagall didn't know proportion, and the Emperor complained that Mozart's music had too many notes. They were all 'found out' and just kept on creating anyway.

Artists at their most creative usually do not seek to be popular. When artists begin to create with an eye to popular success or commercial value, they tend to lose the freshness of their vision, and their work becomes less interesting and often, to them, less satisfying. They refer disparagingly to the commercial projects as the 'pot-boilers' or the 'bread-and-butter work'. So we can see that the person suffering from the Achilles Syndrome is often motivated by getting the approval of others, whereas the creative person very often has to risk losing the approval of significant others or fearing the loss of their hard-won 'popularity', and may well be willing, if not happy to do this. They are careful to be seen to take the 'right' side, creating an impression of always being right by avoiding risk, exposure, true responsibility.

Fear of Rejection Versus Fear of Being Restrained

Let us contrast the creative person with the pseudocompetent. The pseudocompetent person is psychologically preoccupied with achieving externally set standards of competence and fears rejection and shaming if they fail. For many artists the greatest fear is not shame or humiliation, since most creative children have to learn how to survive ridicule, parental disapproval, public humiliation and to live with such rejection. Instead the artist's horror is of being restrained, being prohibited from the outside and blocked from the inside in terms of expressing their creative urges.

In this regard it is important to remember that it has often been the artists (dissidents?) in fascist societies who have challenged the establishment, been tortured or imprisoned or censored. Many have been killed and others, such as Solzhenitsyn, Vaclav Havel and Gauguin, are artists associated with those parts of society most despised and rejected by others. Others concentrate on the 'low life', such as Faulkner and Toulouse Lautrec with their pictures of prostitutes and poverty – on the untidy, dirty, shocking parts of society.

A Desire for Order Versus a Delight in Chaos

Of course we all fear rejection and loss of freedom and we all want order – and may delight in chaos. It is natural that parts of our lives are concerned with *products* and some with *process*.

I am highlighting these polarities, not to suggest that there is a finite line between them but to show how lives or periods of time can often be organized around one of these polarities. Obviously, a few people will achieve (or claim to achieve) a balance between them. However, it is typical of the pseudo-competency orientation to want to achieve *balance* whereas the creative orientation knows that, as they say in chaos theory, 'creation occurs at far from equilibrium conditions.'[2] The very nature of the creative process is disordered, unpredictable and erratic. Paul Klee said: 'Becoming is superior to being'. It was Kant who pointed out that art is purposive without purpose. It is a rare artist who delivers all the time, exactly in the same way, on schedule. If someone such as an actor were to achieve this, he would have achieved a mechanical representation. Our very aliveness leads to uncertainty, difference, and therefore to mutual enrichment even if (or because) it includes disruptive, transgressive and disturbing elements.

When this goes wrong, the pseudocompetent artist maintains the image of himself as an artist without necessarily being creative. Maybe he holds on to superstitions about his own creativity or develops blocks and resistances instead of creative opportunities. One particular counsellor working in an art school found that he encountered very particular problems there due to the environment. He told me:

> Everyone there is seen as creative, and what I do is seen as destructive. It is a strange relationship. There are the stereotypes of artists, with the idea of creativity as a gift, verging on madness. The people I deal with actually fear looking at themselves in a structured way, they see it as the destruction of creativity. They have a lot of creative juices in their neuroses and counselling is seen as a threat.

A Striving for Balance Versus an Appreciation of Life's Natural Imbalances

Creativity and balance are enemies. As humans we may look like symmetrical forms but, in terms of the body's biological processes, to be completely balanced is impossible. It has been found by medical researchers that the heartbeat fluctuates naturally, far from being a clockwork rhythm – and the only time it becomes completely regular is in the short period immediately before a heart attack. Machines are regular, people are not. People keep changing. Creativity can be very offensive to those who have given it up in favour of correctness, honouring of the rules, being 'error-free'. If people (or professionals) create discipline and order and tidiness in their world it can be very provocative and dangerous to have to cope with the kind of uncontainedness, disturbance and unpredictability that accompanies most forms of creativity. Of course there are always exceptions.

Work Versus Play

Creativity is about circles, spirals and waves – not squares – for it is part of the life force, part of the dance of Physis. Creativity exactly mirrors the essentially cyclic process of life itself. Things go round, become fully connected and then melt away and disappear. They fill up and then empty. We breathe in, then breathe out. We become competent, and then incompetent. And, to the extent that we do these completely, the quality of our body and soul's life is enhanced. The recent preoccupation with linearity shown by our technologies and our thinking systems and leaders is against the natural flow of beings.

Truly creative people value the importance of playing. How many adults in our society have the opportunity to play and enjoy themselves at playing, in a non-competitive environment? The willingness to engage in an activity for its own sake, whether or not it passes a standards test, is a hallmark of genuine creativity. People lose this capacity in a standardized society colluding in maintaining pseudo-competence.

Einstein said the following to a friend who asked him how he had discovered the theory of relativity:

The normal adult never bothers his head about space-time problems. Everything there is to be thought about, in his opinion, has already been done in early childhood. I, on the contrary, developed so slowly that I only began to wonder about space and time when I was already grown up. In consequence I probed deeper into the problem than an ordinary child would have done.[3]

I believe that all people are born creative but that, through many of the forces we have identified throughout this book, this natural creativity is interrupted, perverted or damaged. A parent may succeed in getting their child to become an engineer rather than a sculptor – through manipulation of love, threat or reward. A child may decide to suppress the sensitive, artistic side of himself under the pressures of his early experiences, or seeing a friend be ridiculed for wanting to be a ballet dancer. It is significant how many people who eventually became artists have had to fight their parents or a restricting society in the same way. I believe it is very necessary to develop this robustness in protecting and defending creativity from the natural spoiling and fear of other people. Creativity, like happiness, needs courage.

As Rollo May said, every new idea or significant scientific invention will destroy. He quoted Picasso who said that every act of creation is first of all an act of destruction. Destructiveness, or at least de-structuring or deconstruction, is an essential part of creativity. Often when there is creativity there is a mess and noise and it is very necessary to be able to break a previous mind set or habits. Habit is also the enemy of creativity.

One woman at a workshop could not throw any food away, and came to see that she had been using her body as a dustbin. People who prohibit themselves from ever letting go of something or breaking it can end up being totally overwhelmed and imprisoned by such useless baggage. Another woman on the same workshop had an incredible breakthrough in terms of her own art because up to that point she had seen creativity only in terms of making things, not destroying them, and was incredibly frightened about her capacity to destroy.

It is in the In-between Spaces that New Things Can Happen

How can we create a space so that new things can happen in it – an invocation space? Most of the limiting beliefs we have actually sound rational and reasonable. The road to freedom and creativity often sounds irrational, even crazy at the time. Jung considered both intuition and feeling to be the irrational functions of every person. In people whose lives are more under the influence of Physis, there will naturally be a pre-ponderance of intuition and feeling (see the discussion of the different tempermental types in Chapter 3). Of course sensa-tion and thinking are also necessary in order to bring the creative expression to fulfilment but this is another area of creativity.

Our culture places more value and therefore greater re-wards on thinking and logical analysis following an ABC sequence, and this tendency is entrenched in our schools and universities. However, most innovators are not necessarily thinking types because the very nature of scientific discovery seems to be this kind of sudden, dramatic shift. Scientists often tell of inspiration coming to them at unexpected mo-ments, in dreams or in the bath, showing how accidental scientific invention can be. There can be a playfulness and unplannedness about genuine discoveries. Penicillin was not discovered analytically but as an unplanned growth in a saucer on one side of a laboratory, to which someone sud-denly paid attention. It is the willingness to pay attention to the unconventional or to the detail as if it has never happened before that is the mark of discovery; also letting go of the need to control.

An artist introduced his new painting, 'The Carnival of Al' to me during the research for this book. He said the process of painting was like allowing the images to filter through and then crystallize. He would change his mind during the course of the painting about not just the details but the main objects, their positions and boundaries. He found he liked to wrestle with these issues, such as whether to crop a section off one side or not. Images came and went, and the overall picture shifted a lot – it seemed to be building up in layers – but some images went straight on and stayed there. A thinking process accompanied the painting process, not quite in tandem. The willingness to break these boundaries, experience these overlaps, is an important part of understanding the learning cycle and thus of breaking pseudocompetency.

> I work in a place where it is all about keeping boundaries. Doing this work on Achilles, I broke through my own boundary. I did four paintings. I usually paint in threes, but last night I did a fourth. The first one was a boundary; the second, anger locked up; the third, destructive; and the fourth, this one I really like, it's a dance, full of colours.

The Importance of Always Being Right Versus the Willingness to Make Mistakes and Fail

I used to have the idea, particularly of visual art, that paintings came out all in one piece. I was struggling with the fact that as a writer I go through the process of making many drafts. Some writers write clearly from one sentence to the next, but I tend to go through multiple drafts. Usually this is very different from my poetry. I had it in my head that painters had a different life, until I discovered how many painters made many different versions of the same painting, and then found the same is often true of musicians with their tunes. It is certainly more common than I ever imagined for artists to keep revising and repeating their work. For example, Monet kept painting the same scene, and apparently many artists actually throw their drafts away. This was a revelation to me. The same goes for acting. Actors play the same part many times approximating the final performance and then, of course, can still often see how far they fall short of the ideal representation. The same can be true of anyone trying to express themselves honestly – how often have you ended a conversation and then ten minutes later had a flash of what you truly wanted to say? The French call this 'l'esprit d'escalier', literally meaning the spirit of the staircase, for you always have the inspiration on the stairs on the way out.

This is why I call writing an exercise in humility, and I have learned to overcome a very serious writing block to my own creativity. One of my major fears was that, once I had said something in a particular way, I would not have the chance to revise it quickly before more people read the previous version. I realized that I could go on revising and improving everything I wrote for ever, because I was in a continual, often quite radical, process of learning, growing and changing. International feedback gave me some positive responses to my work. I saw one major way in which I was blocking my awareness was the belief that if only I had longer I could write it so much better with the benefit of all the time and experience in between.

I had to learn to accept that there comes a point at which we have to let go of a product, knowing full well that by the time it is in print we would have wanted to have done it better. I now feel more at peace with the fact that my writings are the tracts of where I have been, rather than the markers of how right I can remain. 'He who never changes his mind never corrects any of his mistakes.' I was also frightened that people would misunderstand me. Then I read in Henry Miller 'I write and then they misunderstand me and then I write and they misunderstand me and then I write again.' This was helpful in showing me the inevitability of being misunderstood for a writer or artist. This makes it very necessary to remain in communication with readers for the future. In the sense that any work of art is ultimately what the reader or viewer makes of it, postmodernist thought tells us that the reader creates a text, not the author. After all, creativity is not an end product but the beginning of a dialogue.

The Warrior Protecting your Creativity

Creativity is hard and dangerous work and to do it, we have to be really tough and warrior-like. People want to destroy creativity because if they have become alienated or scared off from all these irrational, destructive upsetting forces, then their appearance is disturbing. They may also be envious of the freedom to create. We need to develop our own warrior skills in order to keep the force of destructive criticism from harming our artistic projects while they are still new and vulnerable in the world. The warrior may seem an aggressive image but is the symbol of protection from the harm of others, of building up immunity so your creativity and flair can survive healthily.

We may feel we need a warrior to protect our creativity when we simply feel tired, but it is important to know that some kinds of tiredness come from suppressing creative energy – it can take a lot more energy to hold in the creative force than to unleash it. This is particularly true in organizations for the middle managers. Many of them feel more fatigued than other groups of workers, because although they are making the same number of decisions, they don't get satisfaction because no creative energy is being expressed, as the senior policy-makers can. Children don't get tired for long at all, they just go straight to sleep.

The Critic Versus the Creator

In all creative work there is a necessary and important duality between the creator and the critic, whether that critic be internal or external. Both these roles have a part to play in the finished product, but they cannot co-exist, as in the famous faces/vases picture where you see either vases or faces but never both simultaneously. Pseudocompetents are critics yet cannot benefit from the critical process, either in giving or in receiving.

We each contain an internal critic or editor, just as we contain a creator. The job of the creator is to take risks, to be original and innovative, in expressing a feeling or a vision in a particular medium. The job of the critic or editor is then to structure and shape that material, to look at it as an audience would. The job of the critic should never be to damage the creator or insult him, although what the critic has to say may be tough. Positive feedback is the most helpful form of shaping and structuring. A poet encountered some difficulty in finding her true and honest voice, in writing freely about matters that were closest to her heart, about sex and intimacy and grief. She found a helpful writing exercise that ended with the advice: 'You are not writing for your aunt!'

Any writer has discovered the creeping paralysis which sets in when you try to write and edit at the same time – it is impossible to do both well at the same time. Each hinders the other because the conditions which are necessary for the one act as handicaps for the other. Of course nothing that I say here is true for everybody since human beings are so infinitely variable. Dorothea Brande has helped writers separate out these two functions – both of which are necessary for good writing. They are intrinsically different, often contradictory processes. People often think that they are only being creative while they are obviously in the process of producing, but all creative acts have many elements and another name for *procrastination*, for example, is *preparation*. See Table 9.2, below, for a list of the two poles of being that also includes the role of critic and creator.

We can all separate out the phases of making and judging, the stages of playing, which is creation, and shaping, which is production. 'Art is not about good ideas' say the critics – and they are partly right, because it also involves much hard work and revision. Everyone needs to learn to find independent play space for themselves that is separate from the parents, whether it be internal or external. Physis does not flourish within a judiciary system; if we consistently think 'Am I doing this right?' or 'Are they going to like it?', we kill it. Creating is finding freedom from the constraints of the collective standards of what is good or beautiful. Why should the critics get all the space? Can we make our own creative voice as loud or louder than the critic's voice? As Mel Brooks said: 'Critics can't even make music by rubbing their back legs together.' Kenneth Tynan

Table 9.2 The two poles of being

Artist	Pseudocompetent
Physis	Eros/Thanatos
Inner motivation	Outer motivation
Fears restraint	Fears rejection
Delights in chaos	Desires order
Appreciates imbalance	Preserves balance
Empty	Full
Creator	Critic
Creation	Redemption
Irrationality	Rationality
Unreason	Reason
Non-linear	Linear
Timeless/time-warped	Sequential/time
Nonsense	Logical/Positivist/'Truth'
Body/genitals	Mind/stroke
Primitive	Civilization
Woman	Man
Immature	Mature
Emotion/feeling	Thinking
Right hemisphere	Left hemisphere
Process	Product
Arts and religion	Sciences
Madness	Sanity
Chaos	Order
Random	Predictable
Metaphorical	Statistical

defined a critic as a man who knows the way but can't drive the car. 'Critics always want to put you into pigeonholes, which can be very uncomfortable unless you happen to be a pigeon' (Max Adrian).

Suggestions and Exercises

• Find materials from your immediate vicinity and within a short period of 15 or 20 minutes make something creative.

Review how you interrupted or encouraged yourself during the exercise.

- Take a clean page and draw a symbol of yourself at your most creative. On the same page draw a symbol of yourself at your least creative.
- Go and find or buy something which you then destroy. (This is an exercise to put you in touch with whether you can use your capacity for destruction in a safe and transformative way.) If you want to, make plenty of noise in destroying it – break a glass bottle in a towel, smash an egg or burst a balloon.
- Draw a bottle around your creative symbol and a specially designed stopper. Describe it elsewhere if needed. Which part of your mother's body does that plug represent? Which of your mother's expressions are most like the plug? Which expressions from your father are most blocking? From your early childhood, which favourite story most represents the blocking element?
- Are you more creative when you are alone or in company? Describe your ideal conditions. Do you create more on demand or on your own generated time? Do you create more easily if your product is to be shown or kept private? Does your creative side need silence or noise (if so, of what kind)? Use the exercise to let your creative side come up with its own answer on how to unblock.
- Write something and prepare to edit it. Go out of the room and come back in a different state of mind. Try to learn to separate these two states. What do they wear? What time of day do they like best? Does the critic wear their hair slicked back or wild and free? Invite the critic in and make sure they come at your invitation (control) rather than acquiesce whenever the critic speaks up.
- Try to find a different space to work in the two separate modes, even if it is a different chair across the study. Don't take the critic along with you to the creative space.
- Describe the ingredients of your preparation stage for creative work. What is real preparation and what is

prevarication? 'When you're in the middle of something, everything looks like a muddle.'

- What is permission to stop for you? Firstly to stop for the moment, and secondly to let go of the project at the end?
- List some ways of changing your mood – it does not matter what you do, but do something different: pick some flowers, speak to the dog – just break the frame for a moment.
- A note on drugs and alcohol: these act as a super-ego or parent solvent. If you don't want to use them, you must find other techniques to deal with interfering internal critical voices. A music composer found that he wrote best through the night because only then were the rest of his family quietly asleep, and his internal critic seemed more active during the day than at night, when his creative voice awoke.
- Making a fool of yourself: go to a shop and ask for something silly such as one brown paper bag. Insist on buying it. Practise making a fool of yourself, experiment with allowing yourself to be seen as clumsy and fumbling. Build up tolerance for it.
- Learn how to defend your creativity from unjust and unreasonable criticism. Realize how not to be affected by criticism from enemies, or friends who are in a bad mood. List some of the most destructive criticisms that you can imagine. How can you prevent or protect yourself from the negative consequences of them? Cherish your creativity, and develop some robustness. Attack with determination those who try and shame you – develop a reflex of an angry response to any attempt to shame you around your creativity and abundance.
- Learn how to deal with interruptions. How do you sabotage your own creativity, either by responding to interruptions or creating your own? How do you interrupt the other creative people in your life? What are your real reasons for stopping their flow?
- Decide how many skins to put on in different situations with different people. Identify where and with whom you need to add armour or skins – if in doubt, remember it is

easier to over-arm and then remove a few layers than to put layers on in the thick of battle.

- Do you put your left shoe on before your right shoe in the morning? Fold or crinkle the toilet paper? Brush your upper or lower teeth first? First become aware, and then experiment with doing it the other way round.

- Exercise your change muscles every day. We can all suffer from 'hardening of the categories' – so it is vital to do something new every day if you want to stay young, flexible and creative. You have intentionally to introduce novelty and learning challenges consistently in your life; even if it is walking backwards in through the front door of your house. Make love in a different setting. Eat something you never ate before. Never let a week go past in which you haven't done something you never did before. Buy one different thing at the supermarket every week; something you would never normally have tried. Swap homes with a friend for the weekend.

- Start longing for your own creativity. If it makes you feel sad, remember that sadness is appropriate in longing for something. What would your own creativity be? What is that yearning about?

CHAPTER TEN

Healing the Achilles Syndrome – Part 1

HOW TO DEAL WITH PSEUDOCOMPETENCY IN ONESELF AND OTHERS

COMING CLEAN

'Odysseus of the nimble wits', replied Achilles the great runner; 'to save you from sitting there and taking it in turns to coax me, I had better tell you point-blank how I feel and what I am going to do. I loathe like Hell's Gates the man who thinks one thing and says another; so here I give you my decision.' (p. 169)

This chapter is about how to deal with the Achilles Syndrome in order to heal oneself and others. In particular it covers the good reasons (or advantages) for why we go on pretending; then reviews the powerful reasons for giving it up. It then gives practical strategies for identifying and defending oneself against the destructive effects of pseudocompetency.

The Advantages of Pseudocompetency

Why do people go on pretending?

Safety Net

People go on pretending because pseudocompetency brings certain advantages. It gets you a lot more strokes from others – they give you support, affection, safety, reassurance. In this way you avoid losing friends whose claim to fame is that they are supportive of you. You get many more strokes for complaining about what cannot be sorted out than by being a problem-solver. On the other hand, your particular area of pseudocompetency may be exactly that you are a problem-solver:

> I used to think that I had a gift of being able to fix problems – a grandiose belief of myself – so I'd listen really well to friends and tell them what to do. A lot of those friends wanted to take that on, so they did what I said and then I also felt better because I was reinforcing my script. One day – I was 17 – a very good friend of mine said: 'I feel really angry with you. You never tell us about you or whether you're depressed or whether you feel about your boyfriends the way we do; you're always listening to us and it's just a one-sided friendship.' No one had ever said that to me and I think the reason I couldn't share with this girlfriend was because I did not understand what a problem was, I didn't think I ever had a problem.

A company director said: 'I am expected to keep on giving and giving – because I can. But I sometimes want to be appreciated for quite trivial things, let alone the major achievements.' It is quite dangerous to give up pseudocompetency in our society. It is safer to create a closed world in which externally imposed standards cannot impinge; perhaps at the office, by blaming the high achieving boss who is seen as unreasonable, or maybe socially, by being unwilling to get involved with people unless you are certain of being liked. In a collusively pseudocompetent society, you are one of the crowd.

People do not avoid becoming competent for stupid reasons. You have a lot more friends by staying pseudocompetent, and you can be a lot more popular. You avoid losing face or being embarrassed. You avoid the risk of trusting or intimacy with others. You avoid the difficulties of taking responsibility for correcting the fault or learning the missing bits. Ultimately, all this avoidance is an attempt to build a safety net against the uncertainty of chaos, and the experience of the void.

The Disadvantages of Competency

Target Practice

There is a lot of pleasure in competency but there are also penalties involved. There is a responsibility when you awaken or support people's creativity that you also teach them warrior skills, in how to protect their creativity. To cross over the frontier from potential to actual makes you a living embodiment of the fact that people can achieve their goals or reach the 'impossible dream'. People may even bear a grudge if others are seen to do this while they are not.

People go on pretending partly in order to avoid other people's envy, for it is a part of human nature that a good object will be attacked for its goodness. Envious human nature tries to diminish or demolish achievement in order to safeguard, rationalize or justify our own unfulfilled dreams, neglected creativity or fearful avoidance of the enormous responsibility of our own gifts.

Not fulfilling your own potential is dangerous. It acts like a corrosive acid. A successful actress once said that when young she desperately wanted to be an actress; she felt as though her life depended on it. But she felt so strongly that she could not bear to go to the theatre, as it so provoked the agony of her own unfulfilled desires to be on stage. The irony in these situations is that, by avoiding or cutting ourselves off from them we stop ourselves from having experiences that could be valuable.

Any champion is immediately put into the position of being expected to win again. They can never rest and often feel they must always perform. People have to be quite strong to be truly competent because if you are good at something, you evoke so much rivalry. A successful businessman said: 'The better you get, the more you activate people's envy and thus their maliciousness – and the more vulnerable you become. While you are pseudocompetent everyone is slapping you on the back and saying: "We know you can do it." The crowd also get a lot of strokes and satisfaction from supporting you. Then when you make it they are no longer so important in terms of being the appreciative, cheering audience and begin to think: "Now you think you can do it all without me" – which is true.'

Human nature is alive with these double-binds. True competency faces other people with what they could also do themselves. Unless you can mate with your own creativity and fulfil your own potential, other people's competency can act as a living reproach to you.

Everyone has 24 hours in their day in which to choose to achieve or not, to enjoy life or not, to keep learning and evolving or not. The truly competent person is out there on his own, and often making his own rules. From thenceforward some people stop encouraging you and some start taking pot-shots at you. You stand a chance of being hurt more in your true self if you are competent, because you have shown a willingness to stand up and say: 'This is me – this is what I created.'

You have to learn to operate from your own judgement rather than the collective judgement, because the collective will crucify and mislead you. It is not always actively malicious, but it just may be mis-timed. It is important to be flexible enough to retain your own judgement but also to be open enough to learn from others. This is what protecting yourself is about. Asking yourself the questions: 'Whom do I trust?', 'What is it about them I trust?' is tantamount to choosing the weaponry for your protective warrior.

One of the reasons for avoiding giving up pseudocompetency is that true competency often leads to (a) attacks from the internal parent, and (b) attacks from the real world, where other people may be very envious. That is what I refer to as the Coriolanus factor: the inevitable collective response of suspicion and distrust of those who are exceptional, competent, enviable. It is envy but it is also grief and injustice. So if there are so many advantages to staying pseudocompetent, what are the advantages of giving it up? As we move through the following healing suggestions, the advantages of 'coming clean' will become clear.

How to Give it Up

There now follows a selection of practical ways of identifying, preventing or healing aspects of the Achilles Syndrome in our own lives; all are variations on ways of thinking about and dealing with it. Remember that at this stage it is not a question of 'Have I got this problem or not?' but of identifying how aspects of this syndrome may be affecting areas of your life, love or work in ways which you would like to change. Many people can identify a few areas; others may find more. At the extreme, you or somebody you know may have crippled their whole personality in this secret but deeply painful way.

You may find one or many more of the exercises useful. You may just want to read through them and be stimulated into considering yourself or people you know or work with in different ways. You may adapt them, obviously, to your settings, needs and aspirations. Remember that not all of them will apply to any one person, of course.

1. Admission or Confession

I have found over the years of working with this material that whenever people have heard the phrase and seen the lead questions or begun to think about the syndrome, they feel very relieved, understood and even liberated. One person described it as 'taboo-busting'. To find out that this is not one terrible, shameful condition from which you alone in the whole world suffer, but that many people suffer it too in many different ways. It is a natural part of the learning cycle. These vital and important pieces of information have freed many people to go forward in their lives with greater confidence and mastery.

> A: The issue of being found out is central and fundamental to my personality. It operates in different places – at work, feeling like a fraud – how much training is enough training. Now, with you as a trainer, you seem to know everything. So you'll find me out!
> B: That's a smart move – pre-empting the public disclosure. People usually hide and hide and hide. You have pre-empted that, you've come to be found out. The payoff has come right at the beginning. It can only get better. However, I'm not advising you do that regularly and in all circumstances.
> A: If Achilles is about vulnerability, then this is taking charge of my own vulnerability by owning it up front, and coping.

It seems the first important aspects of dealing with the syndrome are to recognize it in yourself and to admit to it; be willing to tell one or more people about it. It may feel like an exposing confession, but this admission nearly always leads to people feeling unburdened. Make sure that your motivation is sincere, that you genuinely want to change, rather than blame, 'dump on' or punish others.

The Pressure Cooker

One of the problems with keeping awareness of the difficulties stuffed down inside is that it builds up an enormous pressure of 'steam'. The desire to blurt out to absolutely anyone who is passing can become desperately urgent. Be careful who you choose and how you time it. It is not a good idea to tell your boss in the toilet on the day before your performance review, for example; or to tell your spouse that you have been faking orgasms for the last twenty years when he has just had a heavy day at the office. Pseudocompetence at its worst can contribute massively to life-crisis, for it depends on learning received messages (introjects) which are very alien to the true self, bringing an eventual need to burst out of the old self.

2. Facing the Shame

One of the most important reasons we avoid telling people about the difficulties we have been covering up for a very long time is that we are frightened of being ridiculed or humiliated. In order to change the Achilles Syndrome, we must deal with shame. One of the worst things we can say about others is that they are shameless. It is a way of controlling them through humiliation. It is also very close to envy; the sexy outfit can be called shameless and can be something you would dearly love to wear just once in your life.

Shame is a major way in which we have been controlled, manipulated or coerced into behaving in a way in which other people would like us to behave. Shame is when you fall short of your own ideal or image of yourself. It is different from guilt, because guilt is usually something you feel when you have either omitted or committed some action towards another person. When someone says to you: 'Shame on you', the implicit message is that of abandonment, that you are no longer acceptable to your 'tribe' and that you have lost their love or respect. You have been found out to have a flaw of such a kind that it puts you beyond the pale of that particular society.

3. Being Believed

Every child has had the experience of not being believed when they actually told the truth. Most children have also been shamed for admitting that they didn't know something. Little girl Chozo was the intellectual intimate of her father. She felt like the extension of her father's cleverness and got many messages as a child to be independent and not to ask for help. At table one day she asked him: 'Why does the butter melt on the toast?', he said, not unkindly, 'Surely you know!' Chozo of course learned very quickly not to ask questions again, as a way of maintaining her father's affection and her image of herself. It seems a small event but it became the seed for a lifelong pattern of struggling on her own without asking for help or allowing anyone else to know what she needed to learn or get in terms of help or support. Her father would not believe that she did not know.

How often do we see this happening with our friends, colleagues or children? A little boy says, 'I can't win against the bully' and his father will say, 'Of course you can. All you have to do is stand up for yourself.' A student says: 'I am really not sure that I understand a particular section of this work, that is why I am so nervous about the examination'; and his friends or her teacher says: 'But of course you know it, you always do so well, you must have more confidence in yourself.' The person who is trying to get the help for the covered-up area and is just ready to repair it is so fundamentally disbelieved that they are doubly abandoned. Their distress is not heard, neither do they get the help for which they are pleading (even if in a somewhat disguised way). It is vitally important that you find someone who will take you seriously and believe you. The tragedy is that it is often such a small trigger – Chozo's piece of toast – that can so hurt a life. It is sometimes a single small event but usually these single small events that we remember are examples of a pattern of events that may have occurred frequently in a snowball effect.

> All of this I tell to my teacher and supervisor. Her eyes fill with tears, I feel deeply heard and sense her resonance. I feel and hear my teacher's support in this exchange and there is more, much more to come. For the next few hours I witness this woman offering information about writing on many levels, to me and to the whole group.

When someone next tells you they are too scared to go on stage, believe them and don't hurry them. Remember an occasion in your life when you confessed to having done something wrong or not understood something and were believed by a significant other person, such as a parent, teacher or sibling. What did you do to get them to believe you? Did they know you well as a person, or were they an expert in the particular field? What can you learn from that which you can use in similar situations today?

4. Acceptance of What Can and Cannot Be Changed

People's qualities, temperamental speeds and intensities may be different, but acceptance is something we can all learn. 'If it works, don't fix it.' Some parents may have a fast metabolism and have a slower child, but always be hurrying the child. The child will grow into an adult who always feels rushed. Sometimes in therapy they may discover that the speed at which they have been living is foreign to their first nature. In counselling they may begin to allow themselves to operate from their real speed or intensity, and find that all of life takes on a different colour. For example, couples often combine two very different temperaments – and each temperamental type will also have its own changing cycles within it.

Many women have strong and fast cycles and may believe that these are the 'better' ones, since they can then express their feelings strongly and loudly to their partners. It is only compassionate to understand that their partners may be of a completely different temperamental type – slow and gentle – so that, for these people, shedding a few tears is equally valuable to the big crockery-smashing emotional outburst for the others. This can apply also to organizations or counselling settings in which certain kinds of expression or restraint of feelings are held up as desirable or normal without making any allowance for any variations.

It is very important to separate out first nature and second nature. We use the concept 'second nature' to describe feelings, attitudes and behaviours which we have learnt so well that they have become habits which *feel* like our nature. But even in the idiom of our language, the fact that is it called 'second nature' indicates that the 'first nature' has somehow been lost. I have come to think about counselling and psychotherapy as primarily concerned, not with making people into some excellent version of a healthy human being which is externally defined, but with helping people accept more and more fully who they really are; having them make friends with their first nature, their true selves, their natural inclinations, their own rhythms, their temperamental preferences – which can be identified in hours, if not minutes, of being born.

Sometimes people, family, school, even tend to pathologize people who are different from themselves. That means that they label or diagnose people as 'sick' because they are different from their idea of how people should be or different from them in important ways. There is, for example, the idea that it is 'better' to be extroverted, popular, outgoing, having many friends, being able to make easy small-talk in conversation, and that somehow people are more valuable, nicer friends, better to have at parties. Where does this leave the introverts? It is easy for more shy or introverted people to feel unlikeable, unpopular or de-skilled in social situations because they compare themselves with their happy-go-lucky associates. This leaves them feeling somehow shamed into being seen as sick, wrong, stupid, unworthy, clumsy or unlikeable. Sally told me her new-found vision: 'It's about owning my own temperament as opposed to other people's temperaments, and feeling comfortable with both the benefits and the limits of my own temperament.'

I have had a client who has spent most of his therapy not changing himself but learning how to accept and value the quiet, gentle, thoughtful, sensitive person he truly seems to be rather than trying to break his heart and mind into being the life-of-the party type of personality which he could never be. The difference between introverts and extroverts is biologically rooted, it is in our genes before we are born. All of us can learn to develop skills and attitudes which increase our range of potentials and satisfactions in relationships and in life. However it is impossible, I believe, to change the basic intensity and speed at which our nervous system operates.

Many people tell me that they have discovered they are slower at things than others: or slower than they 'should be'. One said that she had been upset by a friend who told her she was slow to learn from her mistakes – the implication being 'too slow'. She has now found great comfort and relief in knowing that, no matter what speed she operates at, she does learn, and learns well, from mistakes. She also remembers these lessons, and is growing all the time: 'I ask myself now – "What have I learned from this?" – and try to answer this honestly and directly, instead of waiting for the shock or the realization to seep through much later, and often only partially or in a different or disguised form.'

St Francis left us the following prayer: 'Lord give me the courage to change what I can change, the patience to accept what I cannot change, and the wisdom to know the difference.'

5. Identifying Areas of Competency

However important it is to identify the areas in which you are incompetent or pseudocompetent, it is also vital to identify the areas in which you are competent and to learn, review, remember and celebrate the process as well as the outcomes of achieving these competencies. As I said in 'Achilles as Healer' (Chapter 8), it is very important not to teach people who feel stupid. If you really want to do self-improvement, it is vital to start from valuing and affirming the achievements that you have made and the desired changes you have brought about in order to provide the springboard for any other attempt. To feel disgusted about yourself because you are overweight by some external standard or do not know a particular language, and to do some internal shaming about it, are ways of guaranteeing that you will not achieve a permanent change in any of those areas:

> Through accounting instead of discounting (like I did all those years) I am building a stronger sense of self. I'm also allowing people to have a different sense of reality about me and I'm surviving with them. It's really all about owning your sense of who you are or owning your sense of realness.

You have to accept yourself truly and absolutely where you are in order to be able to move on to any other place, and the same applies to dealing with other people. If you can meet them where they truly are, it is much more likely that you can help move them on than if you slap them in the face or humiliate them about the tremendous gap between what they are and what they could be. Remember when we have to think clearly it's tougher, there are more options and choices and we may have to think in a different way.

Hindsight, Midsight and Foresight

Hindsight is the capacity to see and learn from the past. People with hindsight will say: 'Oh, I've done it again.' Midsight is the awareness of being in a pattern of behaviour or beliefs whilst they are still going on. Curing pseudocompetency in ourselves means developing the midsight to see what patterns our life stories are currently following, so that we can start work on discarding or changing them as appropriate. Foresight is the ability to anticipate correctly. Once people develop foresight this brings the self-knowledge to recognize their own, individual ways of being in the world. Pseudocompetency need no longer be part of their 'armour'.

6. Refuse to 'Brazen It Out'

This has partly to do with admitting or confessing (see point 1). If we can refuse to 'play the game' any longer it will break the vicious circle of cover-ups – even if the refusal to brazen it out leaves us feeling temporarily vulnerable or unsure how to continue from this point. We can refuse gently in a spirit of peaceful non-cooperation by withdrawing from situations that invite us to collude in maintaining pseudocompetency. We can refuse actively or loudly, taking advantage of a rush of adrenalin or anger. We can choose whether or not to give our personal reasons for refusing. We can choose whether or not to move immediately to the next step or stay with the refusal for a while. This will depend upon our individual temperament and partly upon the circumstances, such as how many other people are involved in maintaining the syndrome and how long-standing it is. The refusal may seem to leave us with the wreckage of a situation, but out of this wreckage can be built the basis for a more honest and competent future.

> I remember doing my first-year presentation. It was one of those very important moments because I'd done a very very pseudocompetent presentation, so typical of me – it was creative, it was shabby, it was see-through, they were good ideas but they weren't well formulated or well presented at all. I must have decided to take the risk, maybe I was testing out; and the tutor laid into me publicly and it was brilliant. She said 'I hope you don't think this is good' and everybody was shocked. They wanted to rescue me and I said, 'Don't rescue me. I don't want anyone in this group to rescue me, this is good for me, this is good stuff.' She gave me really good feedback, she told me what I needed to do and how. . . and I've never repeated anything like that again. It was a real confrontation.

7. Forgive the Past

A client had a dream in which a huge banner was emblazoned across a pathway saying: 'The past is past'. It acted for her like a signal that it was OK for her now to let go of the burdens of the past, to move forward and outwards on the path into new life. There is a growing school of thought in counselling and psychotherapy which is questioning the enormous importance that has been given to childhood as a causative factor in adult lives and development. More and more people are asking if the future may not be equally important in determining people's lives, and there is an ongoing and genuine concern with the patronizing treatment of adults as children (infantilizing) that occurs as a result of the preoccupation and emphasis on the so-called 'inner child'.[1]

> In high school I was failing geometry. The geometry master was very old and kept going out to the loo every fifteen minutes. I went to see the student counsellor who said we do know that the teacher is incompetent, ill and over retirement age. I didn't want to hear that. I felt: Why am I being blamed for failing the subject? I wasn't getting the help.

Ultimately we are in fact grown up, responsible for our own lives, and no amount of blaming fathers and mothers who were themselves young, probably pseudocompetent parents 30 or 40 years ago can alleviate the freedom to choose and create our lives now. This does not mean that we should not have feelings of anger, outrage or hurt about the things that went wrong in our child-hood it does, however, mean that there comes a point where we need to let go of it and take responsibility for who we are and who we are becoming, and turn a compassionate eye on those who have more responsibilities and fewer resources than we.

> As I think, I have to give up things. I'm constantly letting go of old memories, old times, old relationships – in a way not letting go because they'll all be part of my history and who I am; but they no longer make me ME. If I was back with all my friends and lived the life we used to live, I'd be the me I knew – and that's exactly what I am dealing with now. You say, OK that was one me and now I'm different.

8. Tolerate Temporary Clumsiness

Have patience. We have to understand that clumsiness or a sense of being de-skilled is an essential and inevitable sign that people are in an active learning process. The way in which you react to the frustration of this period is what can make the difference between seeing it as a boring, futile waste of time or a necessary and important stage in the learning cycle. We need to develop this tolerance in ourselves and others, and to create permissive atmospheres for people to make initial errors. This stage may feel like a burden, but it is not – and understanding the learning process means that we can reduce its heaviness and its duration.

9. Allow Yourself to Be Seen to Be Learning/Fumbling

Teachers must be willing to model the fact that they do not know everything, and that at times they must make up the rules as they go along in the search for the best way. If we never see our teachers learning, we will continue to believe that it is possible to jump straight from 'amateur' to 'professional' status in one go. If the teacher does not know a fact, maybe the whole class can try to find the information so everyone can benefit.

10. Give Up on Needing to Be Perfect

Giving up on needing to be perfect takes us a huge step closer to feeling so much better about ourselves that we might just as well be 'perfect' in that happy moment of relief and release from the burden of imposed standards. Who says what is perfect? My perfection could be your idea of a nightmare. A client put it well: 'We're frightened to complete things from pseudocompetency positions because if you do then people will say: "Oh look, you left that out." Whereas if it comes from a competency position you can finish as well as you can, knowing that of course there may be pieces that someone can say: "Oh you left that out, you did that wrong" – but that's not going to lead to a narcissistic wound.' Tara found enormous help and relief in getting some help around the house; 'I felt so happy coming home from work to a clean house that I could have granted wishes!'

11. Name the Fear

Sometimes all of us are tortured and tormented by nameless fears and anxieties, particularly the ones that come in the early hours of the night when we are alone. A client told me he woke up at three in the morning in a cold sweat, crying 'Does anyone love me? Why am I here?' One of the enormous benefits of group counselling or group therapy is that we can learn that many people have these experiences and that we are not alone in our midnight terrors. However, it is very important to learn to name what we fear, and to give the demons titles, nicknames, identifying characteristics or specific scenarios, because it is by naming that we achieve some degree of power over our torturers or tormentors. Kidnappers often try to dehumanize their victims by not using their names, putting a brown paper bag over their faces; generally not dealing with them as people with identities, names, addresses, children, heartaches. It is recommended that people in captive situations like this talk to their abusers, giving them as much detail of their lives as possible – their children's names and what games they like to play, what flowers grow in their garden, how their house looks, in order to humanize themselves and the situation.

In the Bible we are told Adam named all the animals, which gave him dominion over them. By naming our fears and our demons, and identifying the details of our fears, we begin to take some protection against them. These torments are then not just nightmares but rehearsal studios for dealing with the worst that life can offer. Remember that your worst nightmares are unlikely to come true. Even so it is helpful to think about how we would behave or what we would do, and prepare ourselves mentally, emotionally, physically and spiritually for the worst possible outcomes. It is potentially a gift. It is building the armour that Achilles needed, particularly if it also includes a strong and flexible armouring for the most vulnerable flaw.

12. Get Back to the Roots

Deal with the original traumatic shaming incident in which you were exposed or feared being exposed or found out. If you feel that you would personally be overwhelmed or that you don't know how to stand up to shamers, learn from examples which you have seen in movies or read about, or watch colleagues and friends in action. Imagine that you have one of these people on your side, defending your right to make mistakes or to be accepted and respected as a person, no matter how you fail. Watch young children learning to walk, how often they fall and how easily they take it in their stride. They have not yet learned that falling is shameful. They have not yet learnt to be defeated. If a child or young animal gave up every time it fell in the learning cycle, they would learn nothing.

Any kind of accomplishment is in the face of many more defeats and failures than successes, as we see in creativity. Creativity is more like nature's way of dealing with seeds – there are thousands of good ideas which die for the sake of a few which become truly great poems or major scientific discoveries. There is a lot of waste in creativity and learning, and this is the necessary fertilizer from which your project will flower. Edison apparently tried at least a thousand times to make the electric light-bulb work before he had success. A man then asked him whether he did not feel discouraged by all the many failures or felt that these were a waste. Edison said: 'No, I succeeded 999 times in discovering how not to make a light-bulb.' Most creative artists know that. A part in a play may be rehearsed thousands of times for one excellent performance. Those are not wasted hours, but part of the necessary preparations and wastage that forms the scrambled background from which the eventual product will emerge. Perhaps we should not think so much about waste to be discarded but about resources to be stored for future, different projects. People need information about the learning process and how people manipulate others through shaming or humiliating them and we need to defend ourselves appropriately against such attacks.

Study the phenomenon of shame. Notice how and where people get shamed, in newspapers, families, school or work situations. You can see people trying to provoke shame when handling animals, such as rubbing puppies' noses in their own mess; and you can see how the people themselves were treated.

Clear out the roots of shame, confront or escape shaming mechanisms in your own world, and develop skills in protecting yourself and others. Imagine a situation in which you are being shamed. Change the feeling of shame to that of anger and rehearse how you would look or behave angrily towards the people who are abusive in this way.

Another way of getting back to the roots may not involve tackling shame, but instead requires a clear and steady look at the earliest time at which the pseudocompetency troubles began, and an evaluation of the facts. A black student in Britain found that she got a better grasp of her own fear of exams and essay-writing on realizing that she came from an oral tradition rather than a writing tradition. She had an excellent memory and good grasp of the facts but the cultural difference meant that she was not used to setting them down on paper.

Suggestions and Exercises

- Do some diagnosis – identify the areas you are fluffing in, the questions you are afraid of being asked about, the situations you are most frightened of. Then set about fixing them, starting by reading the following suggestions. The point is to make *appropriate* goals, born of appropriate expectations.
- Feedback. Do you accept negative feedback from enemies, positive feedback from friends? Where can you get feedback you can trust?
- Identify what can be changed and what cannot be changed in yourself or others.

- What is the terrible thing that will happen if you both feel competent and are perceived as competent and excellent?
- What have you skipped in the learning process of the area in which you now consider yourself to be pseudocompetent?
- Do you sometimes re-experience the child you once were, or suddenly recognize your own unedited parent in your current actions? Do you experience such changes in others?
- Make a list of the things that, in your opinion, a mature and fully rounded adult does or could do – from learning how to learn to making lists of phone calls to make. Are they all things you do?
- Remember the person in the preface who said: 'This Achilles blurb is just the story of my life'? Copy the points from the book jacket and leave them lying around for other people to see. Don't tell them about it – offer it for them to discover. Be a facilitator.
- What stage are you at with the three objectives which you set yourself at the end of the preface? Are they complete? Did your ideas about the objectives change along the way? Write down the main points of your own learning cycle as you moved from start to finish on these objectives.

CHAPTER ELEVEN

Healing the Achilles Syndrome – Part 2

HOW TO HEAL AND PREVENT PSEUDOCOMPETENCY IN ONESELF AND OTHERS

REPAIRING

Poseidon . . . returning quickly to Achilles removed the mist from his eyes. It had baffled Achilles, who now stared with all his might and decided for himself that he had witnessed a miracle. (p. 375)

This chapter is about how to prevent the development of pseudocompetency in ourselves and others, once we have identified it for what it is. It also deals with how we can repair pseudocompetency in ourselves and others, and also encourage and enhance our natural drive to competency and self-actualization.

In this book so far we have explored the Achilles Syndrome in terms of deficient learning in spite of presented competence or excellence. The assumption has been that we need to become more competent through learning or dealing with the blocks, interruptions and damage to our natural learning cycles. The achievement of objective competency which is matched with inner confidence is usually worthwhile and satisfying. This is often true in our contemporary society. However, it is possible that this assumption itself will have to be changed. To many students and observers of our cultures, our planet and our sciences, it appears that we are in a state of unprecedented transition.

In this chapter I'd like to put forward the notion that we are moving rapidly towards a new kind of society, in which *unlearning* will be as important as learning. Competency will then depend on the ability to let go of previous learning in order to learn new ways of thinking, being and doing which may differ totally from what we have known as competent before. This would involve skills of deconstructing (radical questioning), tolerating ambiguity and uncertainty and, particularly, letting go of much which has served as good solutions in the past. For many of us this may be the hardest part – learning to become competent when we feel and truly are incompetent. Paradoxically this may mean becoming competent at being incompetent.

1. Form a Reparative Relationship

If people have been neglected, ignored, damaged or overprotected in terms of either emotional or educational facets of their development it is important to form a relationship with a tutor, mentor or therapist which will be a healing experience, a corrective or reparative relationship. This may be similar to the original problematic one but in this case both people contract towards and agree to work for a different outcome:

> I just didn't think I could rage enough and there was one time when I really, really wanted to hurt you. I wanted to bite you and you came in and I was in another world but your intervention was so powerful. You screamed and that sounded so loud in my head. You don't do that and I just absolutely felt so safe and contained in my rage and in my fury – but the moment before I thought I was just going to turn into an animal.

Because shaming is form of invasion into relationships (a splitting into 'you' and 'us'), it can only really be helped if you are in a healing relationship.

The following example comes from a client in therapy during regression to a child state.

> 'Take the big paper', says the teacher, 'and some coloured pens. Simply write what comes into your head about our conversation today. Don't worry about form, just get the words on the paper in your favourite colours.' Scribbling and painting the words on the enormous sheet becomes easier. The great void fills with symbols. My symbols, my words. There they are and this woman, this teacher of mine (like no one I've ever known before) encourages me to make more.
>
> I have not yet finished this piece, but I move ever closer to the confidence to do so. As I write now I take joy in the vision of these clear symbols I am making. I have been working on a paper suggested to me by this teacher. For 4 weeks, each day, I have considered the topic. I have enjoyed (to my surprise) the reading and jotting of notes and quotes. I have realized again that I *do* have ideas and enjoy thinking.

2. Transforming the Self or Transforming the Situation

Learn to flex your change muscles. People can choose their attitude to situations even if they cannot change the situation. A vivid example came from a survivor of the Nazi concentration camps who learned to keep a sense of personal integrity and faith day by day in circumstances that reduced the vast majority to despair. A client told of how she had noticed a transformation in herself at a time when she would usually have panicked: 'Normally when that happened I'd want to get onto a plane and just run off. No. I wobbled but then I looked for help. So I blew the whistle when I was feeling like that.'

Many times it is possible to transform the situation. But it is vital that we discriminate and not jump to the conclusion that we cannot transform anything, either the situation or ourselves. There are very highly talented, idealistic, wide-ranging homosexual people within the Civil Service, which can be hierarchical, heterosexual and/or conventional. They may not be able to transform the framework in which they find themselves, but they can find ways of being themselves. You can beat your head against a brick wall – or decide to beat some soft cushions instead. This serves the function of relieving your pent-up feelings and thus prevents ulcers, cancers and other forms of psychosomatic disease, while enabling you (once you have expressed the feelings) to deal with the aggravating or limiting situations in creative ways. 'My sister was jealous of me. She always took me apart when our parents weren't there. I made a decision then not to be affected by criticism It was a bodily response as well, to keep right away from her criticism.'

> I experience pain and despair in this process, but carry with me some of my past learning. I am better equipped to fight the messages which compel me to failure. In the writing, through the sweat, tears and ripping of paper I feel like a brave hero. I wield my sword, I remember my teacher's words from long ago, encouraging me forward, onward against (what feels like) the enemy. My technique is clumsy, I trip and swear and fumble my way forward. As I claw my way through, I begin to understand that I lack a full sense of continuity. I have difficulty connecting one sentence with the next. I remember that I am not stupid and see a mechanical problem which I know can be mended. I am joyous, hopeful and deeply sad.

Part of the skill of transforming the self is learning to stay stable under stress. We can learn to do this by identifying our own bands of competency levels, and utilizing the knowledge of this and of the stages of the learning cycle when we are stressed.

3. Identify Stages in the Competency Cycle

The following section draws on the knowledge about the learning cycle gained in Chapter 3. If you have turned to here first, you may prefer to read Chapter 3 now and then return, because knowledge of the predictable stages of the learning cycle is very supportive to our own learning process.

Learning is a life-long process, not something we do at school and then forget about. Sometimes it is said of good teachers: 'I learnt so much from them without even realizing how much I was taking in – it didn't feel like learning or working hard – they made it easy.' This is true but it is partly about their particular teaching style, and partly about a particular *state* of learning, not about the general *process* of learning. Learning is a cyclic process. It turns like a wheel, or a spiral; or rather we move within it, from unconscious incompetence to conscious incompetence; from conscious incompetence to conscious competence, and from conscious competence to unconscious competence. The three phases are also called awareness, accommodation and assimilation, as we have seen.

Our progress within this cycle may not be smooth, or clear, but definite stages can soon be identified with practice. The spiral of learning starts again when unconscious competence becomes unconscious incompetence. The third phase melts into the first, and we begin all over again. If we can keep aware of the stages of the learning cycle, we will have the huge advantages of (a) always being supported by what we have learnt so far, and (b) of not giving up in the middle or being embarrassed about muddling or getting it wrong, for we know that this is natural in the early and middle phases.

4. Learn About and Accept the Cyclical Nature of Healthy Growth and Development

As I pointed out in earlier chapters, it is a basic motivation of children and developing adults to want to be competent. Achieving mastery (whether of crawling towards the playpen or finishing composing the symphony) leads to feelings of good self-esteem and satisfaction. Learning any new skill or new knowledge brings its own challenges, but particularly its own rewards. The pseudocompetent person, however, wants to go from incompetence to competence without any of the in-between stages. They frequently want to avoid ever feeling incompetent. For true learning to take place, this is an impossible desire. Feeling and behaving incompetently are always a necessary stage in the learning cycle. A trainee reports that: 'I really learnt about making things simple, simple, simple. Even on the first evening when they just had to talk to each other one person left because they got so scared.'

To expand and develop as a person one must always start new things, have new projects, new enthusiasms; sticking with what is known can keep us in a comfortable rut. There can hardly be a final product or an accomplished steady state in any discipline which continues to evolve and which demands of its practitioners continued flexibility and willingness to keep developing. As soon as one cycle is completed, another one begins. In my view this is natural. It is not a compulsive, externally motivated search for mystical perfection, it is more a natural urge, shared by all organisms, to grow and develop and to become more skilled, more understanding and, for humankind in particular, more compassionate. Being in touch with this evolutionary drive in ourselves enables us to continue growing and changing.

We have to go to the toilet over and over again, we have to eat and then defecate over and over again. We have to breathe in to breathe out, in order to breathe in, in order to breathe out, in order to breathe in, in order to stay alive for as long as we live, over and over again. Any cycle of learning of any kind of importance or any genuine competency probably requires the same cyclical process. We are always learning as well as unlearning, becoming stale in the same kind of process as becoming more masterful or more competent in any area of endeavour. In any kind of learning that has to do with growing and changing we can never rest on our laurels. Life itself and the forces which surround us will keep challenging us to the survival of the fittest. This, in the original Darwinian sense, does not necessarily mean the strongest, the most ferocious or best. It does mean those organisms (people, groups and organizations) which adapt themselves soonest and most effectively to changes in the environment are most likely to survive and thrive.

5. Get Teaching of the Basics

Because most people become unconsciously competent in their usual work, they run the danger of reverting to a state of unconscious incompetency – a sort of occupational senility brought on by overt complacency on the part of the worker. This state, of course, is more typical of the type of worker who has no desire to keep updated on his craft or field, who sees no need for additional study once he has learned his trade. Because of this attitude, he is vulnerable to 'unconscious incompetency' and can easily regress to the point where he is, for all practical purposes, an unconscious incompetent. Once we have teaching of the basics we can say yes, I need to know that before I press on. As a student put it, 'People are going to ask me those whys, and if I don't answer the internal why then that is the time when I go back into pseudocompetency.'

In organizational life, the eventual gravitation on the part of the unconsciously competent employee toward unconscious incompetency underlines the need for continuous training and retraining programmes. As in professional sports, this often means that the player must be retrained in the fundamentals of his game in order to make him consciously competent again. And only the consciously competent can train the conscious incompetent, or bring the unconscious incompetent to an awareness of his backsliding.

6. Necessary Regression

Benign regression or rechilding means going back to and then using our inner child ego state appropriately to enhance our adult life. Once we are adult, regressing to an earlier state can be necessary if we are to identify and fill gaps in our learning cycle when we were children. Creativity is also closely linked with the experience of the infant, who is constantly creating a world and explaining it to herself.

Rechilding does not have to be done in psychotherapy, although it can be part of forming a reparative relationship. People can do it for themselves when the environment is conducive to health and growth. It can also occur spontaneously as in the creation of healthy functioning new child ego states; for example, a grown man buying himself a teddy bear or a train set where he never had one as a little boy. He buys it for the residual child in himself, still there, still capable of assimilating new experiences at archaic or previous developmental levels or old ego states, still acting as motivation for a greater fullness of life. A client reports after a rebirthing experience which culminated in an alternative birthday: 'I can energize the old experience or this one which has given me trust in the world.' As the popular lapel buttons say (no doubt reflecting some wisdom from the collective unconscious):
'It's never too late to have a happy childhood!'

7. Let the Teacher In

Allow yourself to be taught. The task of the teacher is to free up the learning process in others. The task of the pupil is therefore to allow a one-way flow of information to come from a teacher and form a firmer basis of learning for the future. The following two examples come from a client in conversation with her therapist.

> I've struggled with learning, because I would think that that's the way you learn, so I would sit and struggle through chapters of books, because there was a real want and hunger to learn but I didn't understand how to do it. I hadn't fixed the other building blocks to get to that point, so I was drowning in my own hunger. I felt like I'd done something to set aside hunger, but it was empty. . . . The reason I can't really learn is because I can't give

up this façade. The only time I could really begin to learn with you was when I could give up my façade, when I felt completely stripped inside, when I really began to just strip myself.

I think my pseudocompetency develops around my existential position that I was armed, which was a defence for feeling bad. It's also tied in with judgement. I didn't feel I could ever really judge publicly or say what I thought because if I did you'd see through it. So I kept my judgement internally for fear of it being seen – inside the internal mess so there wasn't any way for me to find out whether what I thought was twisted or clever or interesting or anything, because I just wouldn't let it out. I'd only let out the introjected ideas. . . . So I censored. I remember in the group I made a contract to ask my questions. That was the beginning of letting people see that some of the questions I'd ask wouldn't always be so smart. They might actually be simple ABC stuff. And then I moved on to making contracts more about taking risks about saying what I thought or felt, and letting you be the censor rather than me.

8. Develop a Relationship with Someone Else in the Chosen Field of Competency

Ally yourself with somebody you respect and feel is genuine in their competency in the field that you have chosen to concentrate upon. Be aware of how they do things and why. Ramsey told me:

I told you about my father and our relationship. Only after about a year did I even think that there was anything wrong with it. And you didn't say: 'This is bad'; but over a long period of time you kept accounting for the real significance of the story. And now I'm accounting for myself, just saying: 'This really happened, this is what went on', and as I'm doing that then I'm owning.

9. Re-establish the Criteria

Build your own criteria by moving the judges from an external to an internal position. Let yourself be the judge of what is or is not right, appropriate or finished. Make the criteria appropriate to you as a person, building on the above skills of giving up on needing to be perfect, but doing what you know will satisfy your own realistic expectations. If it meets those criteria as far as you are concerned, then others' criteria about it may not be so relevant. For example, 'I know it is good writing if the voice is true to myself, capable of being emotionally moving to someone else, and well-crafted.'

10. Redo the Skipped Developmental Tasks or Learning Phases

In psychotherapy, redoing a task that was skipped during an earlier learning cycle may involve age regression; going back to an earlier age. The following example about finishing a project is symbolic of redoing a skipped developmental task. It comes from a client in conversation with her therapist, remembering a regression to age 5 or 6.

> Client: I felt very contained, and very safe and you were with me. It was very important. I could gently show you how jumbled I was before I could show anyone else, and actually you didn't stroke me for my jumbles but you were always very loving about nothing general. I never felt put down. I wanted to complete a project because I loved projects at school but never felt supported in doing them. To be about 5 or 6 and complete a project. I went into the kitchen with my friend Rose and all these children and then somebody came and poured all their juice on our project and I regressed and just rubber-banded. You were in the kitchen and I was going to have a massive temper tantrum, tear it all up, stamp and scream . . . and you just picked me up and held me and spoke to me. You said 'You don't have to do this. You're very angry. Sit down and we're going to finish this.' I just calmed down and felt much better. You helped me mop it up and then you were there with me so I felt protected that the other kids wouldn't interfere. I also felt you were going to help me actually

finish it. So you got the magazines and I finished the project and I was so proud of it. I've still got it and I'm very proud of it.

Therapist: Yes, how many other projects have you finished like your case study?

Client: Yes. It's been very important to finish them. I've always had stamina, but never really in that field.

Note that the client also showed great willingness to learn, and to let the teacher in (points 7 and 8).

11. Challenge the Shamers

Express and mobilize anger against the collective shaming mechanisms in our society, work or relationships. Remember, dream or imagine how you were shamed as a child. Create a safe environment for yourself and then relive it but from a new position of strength. Show your new power of knowing what is right for you and how it works for you. They had no right to do that and you let them know that it will not happen again. Question the judges and, if necessary, invalidate them. Question their ability to set standards in this area.

12. Plan Your Own Healing

The clinical plan for the Achilles Syndrome can be thought of in terms of four stages:

1. Avoiding danger.
2. Sorting out confusion.
3. Conflict and redecision.
4. Meeting the deficit.

These four stages roughly mean: 1. how to keep yourself safe, 2. clarifying what you are confused about, 3. what you are in conflict about, and 4. what you need to change or get – either because you never had it or because your early experiences were not sufficient for reparation.

Avoiding Danger

In working with yourself be aware of whether your inner child registers some danger in giving up your pseudocompetency. Have you perhaps internalized some witch parent who will wreak some terrible revenge on you if you are genuinely more excellent or competent than they can bear you to be? However strange it may seem, although parents usually wish their children well in their personal and professional lives and want to be proud of them, there is frequently some part of the parent that feels envious of the child having the opportunities, care or resources which they themselves never had. People may be more or less conscious of it but it may influence the unspoken messages they give their children about permission to be successful or satisfied.

There is often a real witch message attached to success or achievement, whether it be in love or in fame. For example, the more successful Emma got, the more suicidal she felt. Her family and friends found it impossible to understand, but with her psychotherapist Emma was re-experiencing the tremendous disappointment and envious rage that her mother felt towards her as a wanted, gifted infant who had opportunities and support to fulfil her potential that the mother never had. Somehow Emma had taken into herself an instruction to self-destruct if she was truly successful which was bred from her mother's unconscious envy and jealousy. She had to learn to disengage from this demon parent and create enough safety for herself to be truly successful in her own terms, of course, without eliciting the destructive wrath of her inner parent.

Sorting Out Confusion

The first task is to identify and then clear up any confusion so that the problem can be tackled clearly and usefully. This might involve, for example, getting information if you are not clear about what pseudocompetency is, or what the learning cycle is and how it works. Another term for clearing up confusion is decontamination, in that we rid ourselves of contaminating beliefs, attitudes or inner parent voices that are holding us back or misinforming us. Doing this means we can function more effectively as adults. Decontamination gives great relief of tension and frees up new energy. For example, in a group when one person is consciously competent, and others are at different stages, then naming the stages of the learning cycle releases their tension and thus frees the group up for the next stage. It also demonstrates patience with people learning, who need to allow themselves to be seen learning or fumbling.

It is also healthy and relieving to acknowledge your own confusion, for doing this shifts us from unconscious incompetence to conscious incompetence. Being able to admit to being confused also shows a healthy giving up on needing to be perfect.

Resolving Conflict

Conflict is about the agony of choice: 'Shall I? Shan't I?' 'Do I have to be an engineer like my father or not?' You may experience an inner conflict such as not being sure if you are allowed to succeed in life, versus believing a message that you will never be loved if you do. I had a client who was very bright and successful with a millionaire father. As soon as his bank account got near his father's figure he gambled it away or fell ill. For reasons which were clearly his responsibility, or ones which always appeared accidentally, he could never exceed the invisible ceiling which his father's success formed in his life. When I worked with him in therapy we uncovered the message that he should never outdo his father, even though his own ambitions continually fired him to do so.

Conflict is characterized by an impasse between two opposing desires, two opposing fears, or between different desires and messages which people may have swallowed about themselves, their attitudes or their potential. A typical conflict for people with the Achilles Syndrome is their desire to do well and win external acclaim versus their desire to be understood and make up the important parts of development which they may have glossed over.

Redecision

Redecision involves changing earlier decisions which gave rise to our life's 'script' so that we are able to make changes in the way we live our lives. People make decisions on their own to cover up inadequacies, or to be strong and clever, in other words, without the benefit of a teacher or the gradual unfoldment of the natural healing cycle. These decisions are usually made in childhood under the influence of restrictive conditions, parental limitations, severe threats such as physical punishment or extraordinary rewards such as being treated as the brightest girl in school as long as you don't let on that you don't know how to ask where the toilet is.

These experiences can show up as a feeling of 'stuckness' rather than active inner conflict. Once you have identified the decision that you made, you can make a redecision about those issues. These decisions will depend wholly upon you, your own temperament and attitudes. It is possible for people to decide it's important to succeed in their own ways and in their own time. It is equally important to decide that it's permissible to fail, to make many mistakes and to keep learning and growing, to get up after falling down over and over again. Redeciding covers all areas of life, and in healing the Achilles Syndrome a redecision may be, for example, that you will not let other people shame you again. It may be important for you to shame the shamers or abusers in fantasy by acting out a scenario where you take the part of a just and protective parent or teacher and protest your inner child's right to learn at his or her own pace and to find out for herself without being made to feel guilty, bad, stupid or embarrassed. If that's what needs to be done, you can do it or get help in order to do it.

Organizing to Have Deficits Met

The deficit stage has two parts; firstly, identifying those parts of childhood developmental history which were neglected or neglecting, abusive or over-protecting in terms of the areas you want to change, and then secondly creating ways, opportunities and relationships to provide, repair, recapitulate or heal these; but this time with a more constructive and beneficial outcome. It can also be called reparenting, in that we provide the learning for ourselves that may have been missed out on as a child. Doing this provides us with the information, support or reparative experiences that we need in order to develop more fully here and now. Examples of deficit work would be forming a reparative relationship with mentor, tutor or therapist, acceptance of what can and cannot be changed, and forgiving yourself for the past. A reparative experience might also be the realization that 'I am different from my mother. Being myself is different from being my mother's loyal daughter.'

Curing Pseudocompetency

In training counsellors, it is quite common for them to think or feel on entering training that they have natural intuitive skills which make them good counsellors or psychotherapists. This is often true, but the young psychologists inside them base their intuitive knowledge on the history and dynamics of their immediate family. They may appear good psychologists or psychotherapists for as long as they do not deal with people who are very different from their families, where they first honed their intuitive skills.

There are three problems with this kind of 'precocious intuition': (a) It is the intuition of a very young child, and therefore lacks a great deal of adult information; (b) It is based on a very limited sample of the human race and therefore lacks generalizability to any great extent. There is a danger of mapping genuinely new experiences and different people into the familiar and old moulds; (c) Usually, no matter how skilful these people were in intuiting what makes mummy run and what to do to please daddy, how to avoid grandfather's temper they did not succeed in curing them. There is a deeply ingrained tendency to survive these conditions at the risk of limiting, straining or even amputating part of themselves, their feelings or abilities and very rarely do these loving, gifted, intelligent children succeed in curing the dysfunctional family or the injured or abusive parent. Fortunately, the process of counselling and psychotherapy requires that all trainees engage in the process of psychotherapy themselves. In this process it becomes possible, while valuing childhood gifts and precociousness, to update and build on these awarenesses with information, skills and self-questioning which can ensure greater success and more effective interventions, whether as counsellors, managers or parents.

Suggestions and Exercises

- Value the part of you that was so successful in covering up for so long. It does at least have stamina, resourcefulness and its own form of creativity. What other positive qualities does it have for you?
- Make a list of people you envy and people you feel grateful to. Is anyone on both lists? Why?
- Envy: list what you are frightened about in other people's envy and what it will do to you. How can you protect yourself from this?
- Whose opinion do you respect? Can you judge their competence to implement their criteria? How do you recognize incompetent judges? How do you judge the judge's ability

to set standards in the area about which you are concerned? Identify the criteria by which you will accept competency judgements from the judges so that you will end up trusting their judgements of you.

- Think about all the things or people you fear and write down their names. Then imagine being confronted with them each in turn as the worst that could possibly happen (remember this is an exercise).
- Stay stable under stress.
- Imagine the worst that can happen. What can you do for yourself then? How would you cope with the worst that could happen? How many ways can you find of preventing it that are not pseudocompetent? Find several ways of coping and preventing and write them down. Take out this list whenever you feel fear in the future.
- Now switch into the opposite of fear, which is fierceness.[1] Look fierce enough to make someone afraid of you, and give this fierce look to objects around the room. Feel your power when being fierce.
- Identify an area in which you want to develop competence, and then define how and from whom and when you can ask for help in achieving it. This is about competence in knowing when you need more information, and identifying who has it – and also acknowledging your incompetence in that you need help and can see that others know more or are more able.
- Sort into therapeutic issues, the ones that hurt or you need safety about and the ones you really want to change very soon, and are highly motivated to change. Find a teacher or training course who will teach you in a particular way, for example about becoming physically graceful. Who can work with you? Perhaps a movement therapist can work with you on the way you walk, and increasing your awareness. Don't worry about being critical of teachers, stick with one you choose, even if you don't like bits of the way they do it. Do you feel real with the teacher?
- Create learning experiences to give you good experiences around learning.

CHAPTER TWELVE

Achilles at Large in the World

CURING PSEUDOCOMPETENCY: THE KEY TO A HEALTHIER TWENTY-FIRST CENTURY

Odysseus caught the signal, and having filled his cup with wine drank to Achilles and said: '. . . We are confronted with a disaster, your highness, the magnitude of which appals us. Unless you rouse yourself to fight, we have no more than an even chance of saving our gallant ships or seeing them destroyed.' (p. 167)

Adrift in a Sea of Change

It is more than ever the experience of ordinary people as well as experts in various fields that world changes are happening faster, and in more complex and unpredictable ways, than in living memory. Our natural needs for security, control, certainty and predictability are constantly undermined as institutions go out of business, new scientific inventions flood the market and social and economic conditions fluctuate in unpredictable ways. We used to be able to give our children an expectation of a lifetime of employment, but this may no longer be the case. Many business people find their targets increased and resources lowered, while expectations for performance just escalate. In the words of one manager: 'We feel we're going crazy because we are expected to do what we all know cannot be achieved.'

Such is the breeding ground for pseudocompetency as we face the next century. We live in a world where the old scientific, cultural, religious and political models for 'explaining everything' have lost their ability to inspire; it seems that they had only an interim usefulness. The nature of change itself has changed and will only continue changing, whether through evolutionary development or radical quantum leaps. The quantity and quality of change also seem to be changing. At the same time as the tempo of change accelerates, we notice the rise of fundamentalism in the world. It is a natural human response to such conditions of uncertainty that we sometimes reach for the securities that come from external authority. We face a future that is turbulent, unpredictable and potentially dangerous. We have no idea whether we are able to turn back the tide of the ecological destruction of our planet in time to save it for future generations or avert a massive ecological disaster.

New Perspectives

The call of Odysseus to Achilles to come and do his work properly and competently is going out to every responsible and responsive human being at this perilous time. Our physical conditions have changed so much, for example the holes in the ozone layer. Our mental conditions are constantly changing. The old ideas of Newtonian physics, the laws of cause and effect, the belief in progressive increase in knowledge – all these are under review. Quantum dynamics are undermining much of what we used to take as fact or truth about our physical universe and the way it works.

Professionals who study contemporary culture have noticed that the search for an ultimate truth has been abandoned in many areas. Newspapers and magazines are crammed with the gleeful demolition of any hero or heroine which they have placed on pedestals. There is widespread cynicism and disillusionment among the young people, acted out in the despair and confusion of homelessness, escalating violence to children and old people and a preoccupation with drugs, films glamorizing violence, desperate strategies for survival, mind-softening and time-devouring television, football hooliganism and crime. The world's ills of starvation, plague, war, cruelty and ignorance fill our TV screens.

Organismic Empathy and Environmental Pseudocompetency

As a society we have become pseudocompetent towards the environment. We have 'mastered' nature in many ways. However, we have missed a crucial learning about the approach and management of the environment in our haste to exploit its wealth. We have failed to realize our basic connection with the planet. This promises to be an extremely dangerous Achilles' heel indeed if we do not manage to repair the gap in our learning and develop empathy with the environment that sustains us.

It is our first nature to be connected with other living organisms. The further we get from empathy or fellow-feeling with the rest of the physical universe, the more insensitive we become to the plight of others, whether they be animal, human or the planet itself. Certain things provoke our horror but, by repeated exposure to them, our threshold of tolerance rises and rises and we are less shocked. We become pseudocompetent in terms of our environment when we lose empathy with other living things.

Apparently, if a plant has been injured in the presence of another plant, the surviving plant resonates with the distress of its injured neighbour and even appears to recognize the aggressor subsequently.[1] In human beings this phenomenon can be referred to as visceral empathy, meaning that we feel with the pain of others in our own bodies and our souls. Providing we have not become desensitized, this visceral experience of pain in the presence of another's pain is an organismic healthy response. Most of us have experienced this empathic visceral resonance with others in group psychotherapy situations.

> All the entire green world of plants consists of chloroplasts. If we analyze a molecule of chlorophyll we see 136 atoms of hydrogen, carbon, oxygen, and nitrogen arranged 'in an exact and complex relationship around a central ring'. At the center of the ring is a single atom of magnesium. Amazingly, human blood is *identical* to this chlorophyll, *except* that at its center is a single atom of iron. Thus, our red power is a kissing cousin to the greening power all around us. These stories emerging from contemporary science are awe-some; they are both mystical and scientific. They are part of our learning to live once again in *the cosmos*.[2]

Scientific studies have found that cells have a natural cooperativeness; they seek to work together. Living cells, separated from each other and pulsing to different beats, will eventually become synchronized in their pulsing. This phenomenon has also been found in shops where they sell clocks – the clocks tend to synchronize their ticking. Even in women's dormitories or wards, women's menstrual cycles often tend to coincide.[3] The emphasis here is on the modern scientific evidence for the interconnectedness of all life on earth. In the true nature of cycles, this one has been around several times, beginning with the following statement recorded three hundred years before Christ:

> All the world is working together. It is all one living whole, with one soul through it . . . no single part of it can either rejoice or suffer without all the rest being affected. The man who does not see that the good of every living creature is his good, the hurt of every living creature is his hurt, is one who wilfully makes himself a kind of outlaw or exile: he is blind, or a fool.[4]

Nowadays, this is called the Gaia hypothesis:[5] the idea that the earth is one whole organism, all interrelated with all the beings and conditions on earth and responding to its own internal creative drive called Physis.

Bystanding and the Pseudocompetent Community

A bystander is considered to be a person who does not become actively involved in a situation where someone else requires help. Where one or more people are in danger, bystanders therefore could, by taking some form of action, affect the outcome of the situation even if they are not able to avert it.[6]

In today's turbulent world, it is neither ethical nor practical to maintain that things are not our business, or to deny that we influence outcomes. Nor is it enough to uphold values without enacting them; righteous indignation has had its day. It is the difference between what is called on the street 'talking the talk' and 'walking the walk'.

We live in a society in which pseudocompetency appears to be rampant in government, management, politics, healthcare, world economics, national, international and public settings. Many people constantly complain about the fact that the other people apparently in power or holding positions of responsibility are incompetent (whether or not they are). Yet the complainers do not get involved to rectify the situation. Often they claim versions of the following statements with varying degrees of honesty: 'It's none of my business'; 'It's more complex than it seems'; 'I don't have all the information'; I don't want to get burnt again'; 'I want to remain neutral'; 'I'm only telling the truth (to others) as I see it'; 'I'm only following orders'; 'The truth lies somewhere in the middle'; 'My contribution won't make much difference'; 'Victim blaming' or 'I don't want to rock the boat.' Almost always, responsible involvement (whether it means writing letters for Amnesty International, intervening on behalf of a colleague who is being scapegoated or sending donations to Bosnia) happens in conditions where we are not fully competent – and yet we need to act for our own sake as much as for the sake of the others. Our culture and our world are pseudocompetent with regard to involvement.

Of course there are always costs and consequences to becoming involved. But these need to be weighed against the costs and consequences of *not* getting involved – especially when it concerns our own integrity, the futures of our children and the survival of our planet.

Chaos Theory

The other major scientific phenomenon ricocheting around numerous disciplines, with huge consequences for theory and practice in just about every human field of work or understanding, is that of chaos and complexity theory.

> The first Chaos theorists ... had an eye for pattern, especially pattern that appeared on different scales at the same time. They had a taste for randomness and complexity, for jagged edges and sudden leaps.... They are turning back a trend in science toward reductionism, the analysis of systems in terms of their constituent parts ... they believe that they are looking for the whole.[7]

Chaos concerns the pattern within randomness, which is in itself an aspect of complexity. Chaos sometimes convulses dynamic systems and sometimes simply operates in the background. From chaos often comes a new, more complex and differentiated order. Chaos has often been used as a swear word: sometimes chaos is a sign of incompetence, and the description of an organization or teamwork as 'chaotic' has been a term of contempt. However, chaos theory offers us a new meaning and a new way of looking at options for responding to chaotic conditions: not with an expectation of disintegration or panic at the lack of structure, but an openness to the emergence of novel and more creative output. Thinking about the world in these terms can be considered particularly helpful when dealing with pseudocompetency.

Stability Can Be Fatal

The fractal stimulates; stability can kill. Given the very complex and challenging economic and organizational conditions in which we live at the moment, creativity is required more than ever. Though creativity and balance are arch-enemies, they are essential to one another.[8] The literature of chaos normalizes and actively values imbalances. Creativity happens at far-from-equilibrium conditions; it often needs the stimulus of deadlines, emotional upheaval or a change of setting to flourish. The corollary may be that stability sometimes kills; balance leads to stagnation and 'the middle way' is a state often achieved just before disintegration and death.

Chaos scientists have discovered that predictability and regularity can be a sign of illness. The healthy organism, and therefore the healthy organization, is always out of balance and this process of flux is an intrinsic part of natural processes: flexibility, innovation, the capacity for finding novel solutions in changing conditions. Just about the only thing of which we can be certain is that conditions are constantly changing – just as Heraclitus was trying to teach. If a system is completely balanced, something may be wrong. Machines are regular, nature and organic systems are not. This may account for some of women's traditional problems in a world which has been set up and run largely on masculine lines. We need to give up the idea that competency subsists in maintaining stability, or indeed that competency itself is stable.

Cyclic Awareness – What Goes Around Comes Around

The next important attitude is a cyclic awareness. This is shown in the willingness to do something again and again, knowing that the nature of change experience is cyclic (or spiral). Apparently, we need to enter the void again and again if we are to emerge more fully and completely. Linearity is just one mode of perception. The new era requires that we bring back the right hemisphere of the brain (the non-verbal side of us that works in flashes of images rather than in words) which is our source of creativity, of lateral thinking, of intuition and linking leaps of faith. We may see even leaders take an evolutionary rather than revolutionary role.

Heraclitus said that the only thing in life of which we can be sure is change. Furthermore, the nature of change is cyclical. Everything is in a constant state of flux, and human experience is continuously trying to make meaning from the ever-recurring cyclic interplay between things staying the same and things changing.

How to Fall (and How to Get Up)

'Rolling with the punches' is another way of expressing a willingness to enter the fray, or maybe to enter the void, and to try to survive through flexibility and spontaneity, knowing that you influence the system as much as it influences you. Flexibility in this sense includes the willingness to feel our emotions of love, grief, anger, joy, rather than to suppress or deny them. The skill of falling and getting up, of surrender and yielding again and again includes knowing how to make mistakes and admit defeat – and 'start all over again'. It is this ability to learn from errors that is usually what distinguishes confident competence from pretence or the pseudocompetency of the Achilles Syndrome. People have to learn to deal with their talent, which can never be fully known or understood. The demand of competence is that you know what you are doing.

Letting Go of What We Think We Know

A university professor from Tokyo came to visit a famous Zen master to attain wisdom. The Zen master invited him to a tea ceremony. The Zen master poured the tea into the professor's cup until it overflowed onto the table, but the Zen master still continued to pour. When the professor remonstrated, the Zen master likened his visitor to a full cup. He pointed out that in order to have one's cup filled it needs to first be empty." This story can be very helpful if you have an 'all or nothing' feeling about your own achievements that drives you to perfectionism: 'If I can't achieve perfection, I'd rather not try.' The whole learning process includes building *and* releasing.

So what is emerging as one of the most important competencies of the twenty-first century is allowing yourself to become consciously incompetent again. We will be learning vital skills for handling the void or chaos ahead, which no other generation has had to face. Unlearning is going to be as important if not more important than learning. The cycle which we discussed in the competency cycle will need to be navigated again and again and again from unconscious incompetence to conscious incompetence to conscious competence to unconscious competency again and again and again. We will need to work on our grandiose ambitions to achieve a certain kind of serenity, permanent achievement or recognized position and learn to let go of it over and over again. Stephen Hawking's understanding that things could be broken apart and built up again led him to the understanding of the black hole.

This is linked with the exception to the rule about breaking pseudocompetency. Letting go of competencies is one of the most important competencies to acquire in life. In some ways it is a preparation for a real or symbolic death. Making space for decay, renewal and perhaps rebirth, we face these cycles over and over in our personal lives and in the larger cycles of our civilizations. Life itself, as well as science, constantly provokes us to empty out, to make room, and to begin again in this way.

The enormous implications of these new perspectives in our world have hardly begun to be felt. It feels like a dangerous time because we have to let go of so much of what we thought we knew about the world. In his play *Arcadia* Stoppard puts the following speech in the mouth of the young student, Valentine. I quote it here because it captures some of the 'chaotic' qualities of the competencies that we need and lack as we look towards the future.

If you knew the algorithm and fed it back say ten thousand times, each time there'd be a dot somewhere on the screen. You'd never know where to expect the next dot. But gradually you'd start to see this shape, because every dot will be inside the shape of this leaf. It wouldn't be a leaf, it would be a mathematical object. But yes. The unpredictable and the predetermined unfold together to make everything the way it is. It's how nature creates itself, on every scale, the snowflake and the snowstorm. It makes me so happy. To be at the beginning again, knowing almost nothing. People were talking about the end of physics. Relativity and quantum looked as if they were going to clean out the whole problem between them. A theory of everything. But they only explained the very big and the very small. The universe, the elementary particles. The ordinary-sized stuff which is our lives, the things people write poetry about – clouds – daffodils – waterfalls – and what happens in a cup of coffee when the cream goes in – these things are full of mystery, as mysterious to us as the heavens were to the Greeks. We're better at predicting events at the edge of the galaxy or inside the nucleus of an atom than whether it'll rain on Auntie's garden party three Sundays from now. Because the problem turns out to be different. We can't even predict the next drip from a dripping tap when it gets irregular. Each drip sets up the conditions for the next, the smallest variation blows the prediction apart, and the weather is unpredictable the same way, will always be unpredictable. When you push the numbers through the computer you can see it on the screen. The future is disorder. A door like this has cracked open five or six times since we got up on our hind legs. It's the best possible time to be alive, when almost everything you knew is wrong.[10]

Suggestions and Exercises

- List the things you think are wrong about you, and then rephrase these in terms of positive qualities. 'Stubborn' can also be called 'persevering and persistent'. 'I am intelligent with money, my friend is careful, my enemy is penny-pinching.'
- Resist and go after shamers. Don't allow it to go on around you – as we do that within our world we will become stronger in ourselves.

- Write down those activities, people or circumstances which nourish and support you in transition or void times. People often regress during these times and recapitulate babyhood or the beginnings of life. In the same way, we anticipate or rehearse dying or death when we let go of things, and mourn that which we are leaving behind. For example, you may find it consoling to eat warm mushy food every 3 or 4 hours, get under a duvet or drink from a baby's bottle.
- Make your version of a rite of passage creating a space, a sweat lodge, a cave, a few days in a caravan where you can find the strength to tolerate emptying out in order for new beginnings to take root.
- Make a list of values you would be prepared to defend.
- If your life ended today, what would you like to have done with it?

Glossary

Allower
In TA theory, an allower is a phrase or concept giving a person permission to do or believe a certain thing, or behave in a certain way, for example, 'It's OK to do things at my own pace'.

Anima
The archetype, suggested by Jung, of the inner figure of woman within a man's psyche.

Animus
The archetype, suggested by Jung, of the inner figure of man within a woman's psyche.

Archetype
An image from the unconscious symbolizing elements of the human condition (its physical, mental, emotional and spiritual aspects); such as an image of an old man, a fool, or a goddess. They are typical experiences of all human beings, irrespective of race, culture or creed. Jung also called them 'primordial images'.

Driver
In TA theory, a driver is a learned pattern of behaviour which shows and reinforces someone's script. There are five drivers: 'Be Perfect'; 'Be Strong'; 'Please Others'; 'Try Hard' and 'Hurry Up'.

Physis
'The force of Nature, which eternally strives to make things grow and to make growing things more perfect.'[1] Physis is the all-powerful force for both physical growing and ageing, and also mental/emotional change. It is also viewed as spiritual since it

implies that it is in the nature of living beings and the planet to evolve creatively. I am increasingly convinced that Physis is the most important force to which to pay attention in learning, growth and creativity, as well as in counselling and psychotherapy.

Pseudocompetency

Pseudocompetency is the problem which people experience when there is a big difference between their own assessment of themselves and their assessment by others in their particular field. It is when individuals may appear *objectively* to be able to do the task competently, but *subjectively* do not experience the confidence that they will be able to do it consistently well, without severe anxiety and strain or undue energy drainage afterwards. *Competence* is here defined as being able to meet the demands of the task both objectively (assessed by others) and subjectively (assessed by self). *Incompetence* is here understood, not as a derogatory and insulting term, but as a descriptive indication that further development is required in order to meet objective competency criteria.

Script

In TA theory, the script is an 'unconscious life plan' formed by decisions made in very early childhood or even at birth that affect the course of one's entire life.

Stroke

In TA theory, a stroke is a unit of positive attention given by one person to another and denoting reward or approval, whether a hug, a word of praise, attention, money or reassurance.

Transactional Analysis

Transactional Analysis (TA) is a theory of personality founded by Eric Berne.[2] TA sees the three ego states of Parent, Adult and Child as contained within one personality, and interacting upon one another.

Notes

Preface

1. Maslow, A. H. *Toward a Psychology of Being*, Princeton, NJ: Van Nostrand, 1963.
2. Aristotle *Physics* Bks I & II (W. Charlton, trans.), Oxford: Clarendon Press, 1970, 193a, p. 9.
3. Berne, E. *A Layman's Guide to Psychiatry and Psychoanalysis* (3rd ed.), New York: Simon & Schuster, 1968 (first published 1947), p. 89.
4. Clance, P. R. *The Impostor Phenomenon*, Georgia: Peachtree Publishers, 1978.
   Harvey, J. C. *If I'm So Successful, Why Do I Feel Like a Fake?*, New York: St. Martin's Press, 1985.
5. Castro, J. 'Fearing the Mask May Slip', *Time*, 12 August 1985, p. 34.

Chapter 1

1. Jung, C. G. *The Archetypes and the Collective Unconscious*, Collected Works, Vol. 9 (Part 1), London: Routledge & Kegan Paul, 1968.
2. Conran, S. *Superwoman*, Harmondsworth: Penguin, 1975. A best-seller on how to pretend to have done more and better housework than other people think one has done.
3. Hawkins, J. M. and Allen, R. *The Oxford Encyclopedic English Dictionary*. Oxford: Oxford University Press, 1991, pp. 719 and 298.
4. First identified by Kahler, T. and Capers, H. 'The Miniscript', *Transactional Analysis Journal*, 4 (1), 1974, 26–42.
5. Patsy Rodenburg at the BIIP conference, London, July 1993.

Chapter 3

1. Murray, G. *The Stoic Philosophy*, London: Watts/Allen & Unwin, 1915, p. 43.
2. Bible, King James version, Genesis 4: 6–22.
3. If you are not sure, I recommend the book *Please Understand Me: Character and Temperament Types* by David Keirsey and Marilyn Bates (Del Mar, CA: Gnosology Books, 1984).

Chapter 4

1. Robinson, W. L. 'Conscious Competency – The Mark of a Competent Instructor', *Personnel Journal*, 53, 1974, 538–9.
2. Perls, F. S., Hefferline, R. F. and Goodman, P. *Gestalt Therapy: Excitement and Growth in the Human Personality*, New York: Julian Press, 1951.
3. See Chapter 1, note 4: p. 539 [author's italics].
4. Kahler, T. and Capers, H. 'The Miniscript', *Transactional Analysis Journal*, 4 (1), 1974, 26–42. Reprinted with permission.

Chapter 5

1. Stacey, R. D. *The Chaos Frontier*, Oxford: Butterworth/Heinemann, 1991. Also personal communication.
2. Moult, G. 'Under New Management', *MEAD*, 21 (3), 1990, 171–82 (special edition on Postmodernism).

Chapter 6

1. 'Annette's Toughest Role . . . as Mother', *Daily Mail*, 18 August 1993, p. 12.
2. Wolf, E. S. *Treating the Self: Elements of Clinical Self Psychology*, New York: Guilford, 1988.
3. Cornell, W. F. 'Life Script Theory: A Critical Review from a Developmental Perspective', *Transactional Analysis Journal*, 18 (4), 1988, 270.

Chapter 7

1. Miller, A. *The Secret of Joy*, London: Vintage, 1992.

2. Hite, S. *The Hite Report: A Nationwide Study of Female Sexuality*, New York: Dell, 1976.

Chapter 8

1. Berne, E. *Principles of Group Treatment*, New York: Grove Press, 1966, p. 22.

Chapter 9

1. Storr, A. *The Dynamics of Creation*, Harmondsworth: Pelican, 1986 (first published 1972).
2. Gleick, J. *Chaos: Making a New Science*, London: Heinemann, 1989.
3. Seelig, K. *Albert Einstein*, Zurich: Europa, 1954, p. 71.

Chapter 10

1. Hall, J. *The Reluctant Adult: An Exploration of Choice*, Bridport: Prism, 1993.

Chapter 11

1. Grateful acknowledgement to Muriel James for this excellent exercise.

Chapter 12

1. Watson, L. *Supernature*, London: Coronet, 1974.
2. Fox, M. *Original Blessing*, New York: Bear, 1983, p. 2 of 'Afterword'.
3. Leonard, G. *The Silent Pulse*, New York: Dutton, 1978.
4. Murray, G. *The Stoic Age*, London: Allen & Unwin, 1915, p. 37.
5. Lovelock, J. E. *Gaia: A New Look at Life on Earth*, Oxford: Oxford University Press, 1979.
6. Clarkson. P. 'Bystander Games', *Transactional Analysis Journal*, 23 (2), 1993, also the subject of a book in press (Routledge).
7. Gleick, J. *Chaos: Making a New Science*, London: Heinemann, 1989, p. 5.

8. See Zohar, D. *The Quantum Self*, London: Bloomsbury, 1990.
9. Reps, P. *Zen Flesh, Zen Bones*, Harmondsworth: Penguin, 1971 (first published 1957).
10. Stoppard, T. *Arcadia*, London: Faber, 1993, pp. 47–8.

Glossary

1. Berne, E. *A Layman's Guide to Psychiatry and Psychoanalysis*, Harmondsworth: Penguin, 1981, p. 98 (first published in America as *The Mind in Action*, 1947).
2. For an introduction see his book, *Transactional Analysis Psychotherapy: The Classic Handbook to Its Principles*, New York: Souvenir Press, 1961.

Further Reading

Chapter 1

Cavendish, R. (ed.) *Mythology: An Illustrated Encyclopedia*, Black Cat/Macdonald: London, 1987.

Graves, R. *The Greek Myths*, vols 1 and 2, Harmondsworth: Pelican, 1986 (first published 1955).

Guirand, F. (ed.) *New Larousse Encyclopedia of Mythology* (R. Aldington and D. Ames, trans.), Twickenham: Hamlyn, 1987 (first published 1959).

Jung, C. G. 'Archetypes of the collective unconscious', pp. 3–41 in Sir H. Read, M. Fordham, G. Adler and W. McGuire (eds), *The Collected Works of C. G. Jung*, vol. 9 part 1 (R. F. C. Hull, trans.), London: Routledge & Kegan Paul, 1968 (first published 1954).

Chapter 2

Huxley, L. A. *You Are Not the Target*, Hollywood, CA: Wilshire, 1963.

James, M. and Jongeward, D. *Born to Win: Transactional Analysis with Gestalt Experiments*, Reading, MA: Addison-Wesley, 1971.

Sarnoff, D., with Moore, G. *Never Be Nervous Again*, London: Century, 1987.

Chapter 3

Berke, J. H. *The Tyranny of Malice*, London: Simon & Schuster, 1989.

Bradshaw, J. *Homecoming*, London: Piatkus, 1991.

Cornell, W. F. 'Life Script Theory: A Critical Review from a Developmental Perspective', *Transactional Analysis Journal*, 18 (4), 1988, 270–82.

Nathanson, D. L. (ed.) *The Many Faces of Shame*, New York: Guilford, 1987.

Thomas, A. and Chess, S. *The Dynamics of Psychological Growth*, New York: Brunner/Mazel, 1980.

Chapter 4

Rosenthal, R. and Jacobson, L. *Pygmalion in the Classroom: Teacher Expectations and Pupils' Intellectual Development*, New York: Holt Rinehart & Winston, 1968.

Vaillant, G. *Adaptation to Life*, Boston: Little, Brown, 1977.

White, R. W. 'Motivation Reconsidered: The Concept of Competence', *Psychological Review*, 66, 1959, 292–333.

Chapter 5

Bonds-White, F. 'The Special It: The Passive Aggressive Personality', *Transactional Analysis Journal*, 14 (2), 1984, 124–30 (Part 1), and 14 (3), 1984, 180–9 (Part 2 – Treatment).

Clarkson, P. 'A Small Kitbag for the Future', *MEAD*, the Journal of the Association of Management Education and Development (in press).

Peter, L. J. *The Peter Pyramid: Or, Will We Ever Get the Point?*, London: Allen & Unwin, 1986.

Senge, P. M. *The Fifth Discipline: The Art and Practice of the Learning Organization*, London: Century, 1990.

Chapter 6

Anthony, E. J. and Cohler, B. J. (eds) *The Invulnerable Child*, New York/London: Guilford, 1987.

Axline, V. M. *Dibs: In Search of Self*, Harmondsworth: Penguin, 1973 (first published 1964).

James, M. *It's Never Too Late to be Happy: The Psychology of Self-Reparenting*, Reading, MA: Addison-Wesley, 1985.

Roberts, D. L. *Lumps and Bumps (A Children's Book for Parents and a Parents' Book for Children)*, Dallas, TX: D. L. Roberts, 1992.

Stern, D. N. *The Interpersonal World of the Infant: A View from Psycho-analysis and Development Psychology*, New York: Basic Books, 1985.

Chapter 7

Anand, M. *The Art of Sexual Ecstasy: The Path of Sacred Sexuality for Western Lovers*, London: Aquanan/Thorso, 1990.
Bach, G. R. and Wyden, P. *The Intimate Enemy: How to Fight Fair in Love and Marriage*, New York: Avon, 1968.
Clarkson, P. 'Dilemmas of Difference (Differentiating Couples Therapy Issues for Intervention, Negotiation, Separation or Celebration)', *Journal of Couples Therapy*, 3 (4), 1992, 75–94.
Clarkson, P. 'Facets of the Dance', *Journal of Couples Therapy*, 2 (3) 1, 1991, 71–82.
Fromm, E. *The Art of Loving*, London: HarperCollins, 1985 (first published 1957).
Howell, E. and Bayes, M. (eds) *Women and Mental Health*, New York: Basic Books, 1981.
Tannen, D. *You Just Don't Understand: Women and Men in Conversation*, London: Virago, 1991.
Wolf, N. *The Beauty Myth*, London: Chatto & Windus, 1990.

Chapter 8

Clarkson, P. and Gilbert, M. 'The Training of Counsellor Trainers and Supervisors', in *Counselling, Training and Supervision in Action* (eds W. Dryden and B. Thorne), London: Sage, 1991, pp. 143–69.
Kopp, S. B. *If You Meet the Buddha on the Road, Kill Him!*, Palo Alto, CA: Science and Behavior Books, 1972.
Kottler, J. A. *On Being a Therapist*, San Francisco: Jossey Bass, 1986.
Malcolm, J. *Psychoanalysis: The Impossible Profession*, London: Pan, 1982.
Rippere, V. and Williams, R. (eds) *Wounded Healers: Mental Health Workers' Experiences of Depression*, Chichester: Wiley, 1985.

Chapter 9

Brande, D. *Becoming a Writer*, London: Papermac, 1980.
Chadwick, W. and de Courtivron, I. (eds) *Significant Others: Creativity and Intimate Partnership*, London: Thames & Hudson, 1993.
Dillard, A. *The Writing Life*, New York: HarperCollins, 1989.
Koestler, A. *The Act of Creation*, London: Arkana, 1989.

May, R. *The Courage to Create*, New York: Bantam, 1985 (first published 1975).
Sunderland, M. *Draw on Your Emotions*, London: Winslow, 1993.

Chapter 12

Anderson, W. T. *Reality Isn't What It Used to Be*, San Francisco: Harper & Row, 1990.
Bridges, R. *Transitions: Making Sense of Life's Changes*, Reading, MA: Addison-Wesley, 1984 (first published 1933).
Briggs, J. and Peat, F. D. *Turbulent Mirror*, New York: Harper & Row, 1989.
Clarkson, P. 'The Bystander Role', *Transactional Analysis Journal*, 17 (3), 1987, 82–7.
Clarkson, P. 'Bystander Games', Transactional Analysis Journal, 23 (3), 1993, 158–72.
Gleick, J. *Chaos: Making a New Science*, London: Heinemann, 1988.
Watts, A. W. *The Book on the Taboo Against Knowing Who You Are*, New York: Collier, 1967.
Zohar, D. *The Quantum Self*, London: Bloomsbury, 1990.

Index